The
Last Matchmaker

Willie, his sisters Delia and Elizabeth and their father, Henry Daly.

The
Last Matchmaker

The heart-warming **true story** of the
man who brought love to Ireland

WILLIE DALY

with PHILIP DODD

SPHERE

First published in Great Britain in 2010 by Sphere
Reprinted 2010

Copyright © Willie Daly and Anne Lanier 2010

By Willie Daly with Philip Dodd
Edited by Anne Lanier

The moral right of the author has been asserted.

A CIP catalogue record for this book
is available from the British Library.

Hardback ISBN 978-1-84744-302-1
C Format ISBN 978-1-84744-303-8

Typeset in Garamond by M Rules
Printed and bound in Great Britain by
Clays Ltd, St Ives plc

Papers used by Sphere are natural, renewable and
recyclable products sourced from well-managed forests and certified
in accordance with the rules of the Forest Stewardship Council.

Sphere
An imprint of
Little, Brown Book Group
100 Victoria Embankment
London EC4Y 0DY

An Hachette UK Company
www.hachette.co.uk

www.littlebrown.co.uk

Author's note

To preserve the magic, protect the innocent and bamboozle the guilty, I have changed a number of names, places, dates and minor details. Apart from that everything is as I remember it.

I dedicate this book to my grandfather, who enjoyed his matchmaking; to my father, who quietly continued the family tradition; to my children, who might yet; and to all the couples I have brought to the altar.

Contents

Introduction

I am in Lisdoonvarna, sitting in my office just inside the entrance of the Matchmaker pub, listening to the hubbub of high spirits and anticipation spilling out from the bar next door and the street outside. It is the end of a long night, the third Friday of the town's annual Matchmaking Festival, the busiest month of my own year. It has been mayhem, pure mayhem, a non-stop stream of fellas and girls asking me to find them their perfect match. Now it's time to wind down. Have a drink. Tell a story, or three.

I've been here since early afternoon, watching young men and women checking in to the hotels along the main street and checking out each other . . . suitcases on wheels, different accents, such laughing and talking. Food vans and stalls, lorries delivering beer and at least five fortune tellers; a bustle of activity beneath the bunting that decorates the street. People walking up and down, in and out of the different pubs, the music blaring, gaggles of girls shouting from one side of the street to the other, the men whistling at the girls, the sound of high heels on the pavement.

Taxis pull up all day long, the drivers calling out, 'Willie, I have a carload of girls here all looking for husbands.'

'That's no problem,' I always answer back, thinking about all the different generations who have come here to Lisdoonvarna in search of romance. I know that not every one of them will discover the love of their life here, but they will certainly find plenty of fun and great dancing, will meet loads of people young and old and make friends for life.

I've met many familiar faces tonight, including Pat and Fiona, a local couple I matched only last year; and Jan, from Brussels, in his fifties, back for his fifth year at the festival, ready and willing to try again. As I made my way through the crowd, shaking hands, a young lad grinned at me – 'I feel tonight's the night, Willie' – and seeing how radiant and happy he and his friends looked, I said, 'I feel it too.' I'd bumped into my old friend Mary as well. She is always looking out for a tall, good-looking young fella, and said to me, 'Willie, I'm back for another man this year.'

'Mary,' I replied, 'you've more boyfriends than Elizabeth Taylor!'

And so the magic that is Lisdoonvarna continues.

Now I am ready to call it a night. I close the faded brown ledger that my father and grandfather used when they were matchmakers too. Amy and Aisling, the two girls who help me keep track of all the matches at the festival, start going through the notes we jotted down whenever we had a moment to ourselves.

But a matchmaker's work is never done. A couple of lads from the bar have wandered into my little matchmaking 'office' to see if I am still open for business. They are both good fellas, Denny and Brian, farmers I have known for many a year. I wave them in, and they sit down with their pints next to Kathleen, who flew in to Shannon from Boston only yesterday, travelling back to the land of her ancestors to look for romance.

I've been trying to match Kathleen up all evening, and she has popped back towards the end of all the gaiety to let me know that there's a glimmer of one or two possibilities floating through the September-night air. As it's clear I won't get away for a while, I decide to tell the story of Tommy the quiet man.

Tommy was a bus driver, and a man who had no interest in conversation. Though he was so quiet, he was very hand-some, an Irish version of Paul Newman.

One day, Tommy was sitting at his regular table in Cullinan's. The landlord, Denny Cullinan, asked Tommy whether he had had a good day. He replied, 'The best day I ever had.' Denny was curious about this remark, and when he saw his own wife later, asked her what had happened since the pub opened. She said, 'There was only one other man in the bar today, that's Martin Elroy, and he's deaf and dumb. Martin and Tommy bought drink for each other all day. The pair of them never said a word, just gave each other a nod.' That was Tommy's idea of the best day he ever had.

Now the prospect of the Lisdoonvarna festival always brought a smile to Tommy's face. People would often ask me, 'Willie, can you find a wife for Tommy?' I never said yes or no; I respected his quietness. But one day Tommy broke his silence. When Lisdoonvarna was mentioned, he said with a big smile, 'You must find herself for me.'

'I will, Tommy,' I said, 'I will.'

My mind started going through my list of ladies and wondering who would suit Tommy. I didn't feel I could ask him what type of girl he liked. I knew that if I pushed him he'd say, 'Ah, it's OK, I won't bother,' or 'I don't mind what she looks like, if she minds the house and cooks a small bit.' So I decided I would bring a choice for him. Four girls from the festival had called over to my house, as they often do. They were grand country girls, all working in Dublin and used to plenty of the city's night-life. Many girls head for the city in their late teens and by the time they are approaching thirty have grown tired of the excitement and are ready to settle down and get married. They make great wives and value a good man – a country man. I asked the girls to come out with me to see Tommy.

As we approached Tommy's house he was outside cleaning out the cow house, for as well as driving the bus he had a little farm looking out to sea. I had never seen him out of his bus driver's uniform, which he looked good in. Here on the farm he was wearing wellingtons, with his shirtsleeves rolled up and a four-prong fork in his hand. He looked the part. He invited us in for tea and surprised us by serving some porter cake he had left over from Christmas on a nice set of Delft plates.

Tommy was unassuming, which is always a charming quality. Of the four girls, one, Susan, was equally quiet and never spoke, Bridget talked a bit, Mary a good bit and Martina never stopped talking. She also laughed a lot and made everyone else laugh as well. Susan started washing the dishes and Mary picked up a broom and swept the floor. I called Tommy aside and said, 'What do you think of the girls?'

He replied, 'Isn't Martina lovely? I've had enough of silence in this house.'

'You're so right, Tommy,' I said.

Martina and Tommy got married. I think Martina talks to herself when Tommy goes to the pub! She didn't try to change his habit of drinking most of his free time, though it's not *all* the time: he and Martina do have twelve children.

Suddenly I feel a hefty hand slap down on my shoulder. 'Willie Daly, you old devil, how the hell are you? It's great to see you here, in your own matchmaking office. I couldn't believe it when I was walking down the street and I saw you through the window surrounded by gorgeous girls and fine fellas. You looked like a guru.'

It's none other than Gerry Flaherty. Gerry used to be a regular at the festival, famous for asking women to marry him practically as soon as he met them, as he knew they would never say yes that early. He thought he was immune. Then one year I tipped the wink to a young German lass, and when Gerry asked her if she'd marry him she said yes straight away. He turned on the spot and ran away like a champion greyhound that night. We hadn't seen him back at Lisdoonvarna for several years. I heard he'd been working over in the States.

'So you came back, Gerry. After all that hard work I put in finding you a beautiful German girl, and you disappeared without trace. Have you come back to try again?'

'That I have, Willie, that I have. I think I'm ready to take the plunge. Do you know where I might find a girl?'

'Now let me see,' I say, messing with him, 'do you think that's likely in a town that's full of a couple of thousand single women who are here for fun and romance and ready to meet a good man?'

'Go on, Willie, work your charms for me.'

I look over at Kathleen, and something clicks in my thoughts. 'Well, we've finished for tonight, but why don't you pull up a chair, get us a few pints and we'll talk about all the things you've been up to in the old US of A. And I'll see if I still have the knack. Maybe those computer-dating sites haven't seen me off just yet.'

'Now come on, Willie, don't go underestimating yourself,' says Brian, one of the two farmers sitting round the table.

Kathleen cuts in. 'It's true. I've tried everything,' she says, 'speed dating, blind dates, dot coms, you name it – not one of them has worked for me. I want somebody to help me who won't just add me on to a database or have me fill in a twenty-page questionnaire. How can you say what kind of man you're looking for when you don't even know that yourself? That's why I came over to Ireland. Come on, everyone's told me you're the man, Willie. They call you the last matchmaker, the mender of hearts, the horse whisperer of romance.'

'They do that.'

'Now don't go giving him any more highfalutin ideas.' This is Aisling, who's finished putting all the matchmaking notes together, and always does a good job of keeping me under control and in my place.

'But I want to know,' says Kathleen as Gerry arrives back with a round of drinks. 'What is the secret of matchmaking?'

'Well, if I knew that,' I reply, 'I would bottle it and sell it like holy water! But since we're all here and sitting good and snug, I can tell you a few stories about my life and some of the people I've matched, and we'll have a laugh along the way.'

'That's grand, Willie,' says Aisling, sharp as a pin as ever, and she turns to Kathleen. 'But don't believe a word he says!'

1
A Child of County Clare

I was born to be a matchmaker. Willie Daly, the son of Henry Daly the matchmaker, and grandson of William Daly the matchmaker before him. It's in my blood.

Each morning, as I step out from my farmhouse to take in a broad lungful of that clear, cool air we are blessed with in County Clare, I always spare a moment to glance over, across the sally-bushes and the hedgerow of blackthorn, at the small stone cottage that stands next door. For that is the house where I was born six decades and a little more ago, up here in the valley they call Ballingaddy, or Baile an Gadaíhe, 'the home of the thief', some long-forgotten scoundrel.

There I was born, on 1 April 1943, a birthday that's hard to forget! At least that is the day I was reckoned to be born on, because there is a fair amount of uncertainty about the precise date. In truth, there were perhaps eight or ten of us born in the parish that year who could never be sure about our exact age.

Now, it was the local priest's responsibility to keep a record of all the births in the parish. At the time most children were born at home, not in hospital, so there were very few detailed medical records, and no obligation to register the birth as we have to now. The priest oversaw the christening, which would take place shortly after the baby was born. The belief was that if a child died without being christened, they would be trapped in limbo for the rest of eternity. I remember hearing friends of my parents saying how important it was to get the ceremony done quickly for fear of the child dying beforehand; infant mortality was all too high.

The priest we had at the time I was born, one Father Ford, was by all accounts a lovely man and young enough, so his memory should have been in fine fettle, but he was very fond of the drink. He would perform the christening, ask the parents for the date of birth of the newborn, jot it down on a scrap of paper and stuff the note in his top pocket. But then he'd forget to enter it straight away into the book that contained the parish records. And by the time he did get round to writing in the dates, the original piece of paper would have long been thrown away. I think the Father must have used a fair amount of imagination and guesswork to fill in the ledger, which is why those of us born while he was our priest never knew for certain our correct date of birth.

Mind you, there are some people who are happy to draw a veil of uncertainty over their true age. When I was about twenty-five or so, I received a letter from a lovely girl called Ida. I'd known her when we were both at school together, and later she upped sticks and moved over to London. 'Willie,' she wrote, 'I'm getting married soon, to an Englishman. My husband-to-be is a fair bit younger than me. Do you think you could help make me a little younger than I actually am?' Since there were no official records, the need to confirm somebody's age was a question that occasionally cropped up, though only once in a very blue moon. We would then organise half a dozen people to get together and agree that such a one was this or that age before drawing up a little affidavit for them to use for whatever purpose suited them.

So on this occasion I rounded up two or three fellas who had also known Ida and invited them to meet me in the pub in Kilshanny up the road. I knew that Ida was at least four or five, maybe even six years older than me. But I kept saying to the other guys, 'When I was going to school she was probably two classes younger than me,' trying to knock a good seven or eight years off her age.

However, one of the others in the group, an older man than me, was proving very tricky. He worked for the council and was something of a stickler for detail. He insisted that Ida had actually been a class ahead of him, which was doubtless true. This debate went on for quite a while. We must have stayed in the pub for four or five hours. I simply couldn't convince him, and he was refusing to budge, so we agreed to meet again the following night.

The next evening I made sure I was the one buying the drinks, because I knew that if your man got drunk enough he would eventually agree with me. As time ticked on, he kept checking his watch.

'I need to get off, lads,' he'd say, 'I have to be in the office early tomorrow.'

Finally I had a brainwave. 'You're mistaken,' I said. 'You're thinking about Ida's sister; there were five or six sisters in that family, don't you remember? Ida was one of the youngest ones.' That way I planted a hint of confusion in his mind. And finally, thank goodness, with the help of several more pints (and a dash of poteen from a bottle in my pocket) to enhance the befuddlement, he gave in and agreed with me. We all duly signed the note confirming that Ida was twenty-three years old, and sent her the document.

Another twenty-five years passed, and Ida sent me another letter. This time she wrote, 'Willie, my circumstances have changed. My husband David died recently. Financially I'm not well off and I know that I must be very close to pension age. Could you have another of those meetings and make me ten years older . . .?'

So as I'll jokingly say, I *think* I know how old I am. It would be lovely to believe I might be younger than I thought! And isn't there an advantage in having some leeway in your life, a little bit of give and take?

Nothing is ever too precise in these parts of County Clare. Depending which road you arrive by, you might find a signpost to Ennistymon or Ennistimon, to Corofin or Corrofin, Lahinch or Lehinch. The other morning, some youngsters over on holiday from Germany came up to the farm to go riding. They said they couldn't stay long as they had to drive across country to be at a hotel for midday. 'Don't rush,' I told them. 'That hotel will be disappointed to see you on time; they'll tell you to come back in two hours.' I was joking with them, but it was the truth. We operate in our own time zone here.

If you've never been to County Clare, then let me invite you over.

The view from my farmhouse is the very one I saw as a child. Over centuries the folds and fields of this valley have rolled gently down towards the sea, where the swell of the Atlantic batters the famous Cliffs of Moher. Ballingaddy lies out on the west coast of Ireland, nestling beneath the rugged limestone outcrops of the Burren. Five miles away as the scald-crow flies is the village of Doolin, where you'll hear the finest jig and reel sessions in this corner of Ireland. And from Doolin Pier the ferry boats head out to the Aran Islands, which Seamus Heaney called 'three stepping stones out of Europe' – next stop, America.

Even though I have lived nowhere else but here, I have never stopped thinking what a truly gorgeous land this is, a magical mix of the stark landscape of the Burren with the soft emerald of the rolling meadows. There is a great sense of peace, the quiet of the early mornings broken only by the cries of the seagulls or the clip-clopping hooves of horses out on a walk, though if you listen hard you can always catch a hint of the constant raucous roar of those pounding waves. There is definitely something special carried in upon that sea breeze, something in the waters, that helps the smallest seed of love flourish.

I have always maintained that if you're lucky enough to be born in County Clare, you can't help but be blessed with a romantic soul, or else you must have been born with a heart carved out of Burren stone.

My own heart is certainly here. This is where I learnt to walk, to ride, to laugh and sing, to play the tin whistle, to pray, to dream – and to fall in love and help others find love. Here among the fields and along the lanes that lead down towards our little town of Ennistymon nearby and across to Lisdoonvarna, home of the great Matchmaking Festival each September.

Oh, there have been changes, of course. The jaunting cars and governess carts we rode to town in have long been replaced by motor cars and vans. The candles and oil lamps I learnt to read by are gone, although electricity only came to the valley forty years ago. The roads that were once a treacherous combination of pot-holes, flints and stones have been tarred over. But I have plenty of reminders of those days. My grandfather's jaunting car is safely stored in the tack room next door, there is an old double oil light on the wall of my kitchen, and a rough dirt lane leads up to the old farmhouse where I first drew breath and which has been standing on this hillside since the seventeenth century.

I was the baby of my family. I had two older sisters, Delia and Elizabeth, and there was also my half-brother Michael – my mother had been widowed a few years before she met my father. My mother had a marvellous love for us all; and although my father was an awfully quiet man, we always knew he loved us deeply. There was a great sense of security to be growing up in a loving home with adoring parents.

Beyond the turn of the road was my intrigue. Before I could walk I could see down to a turn of the road by our house. In my imagination, beyond there stretched endless mystery and magic. As my life did unfold and unravel, I was never going to let anything stand in the way of discovering all that magic.

At first I didn't venture very far. I would go down to the little river that runs through the valley with my sisters whenever they organised picnics and tea parties by its banks. It was a slow enough river, only a stream, a trickle much of the time. As youngsters we used to block a part of it with stones, so we could go and have a swim in the little pond we created.

Then I started exploring a little more, usually going out with my half-brother. Michael was some six or seven years older than me, and a great adventurer, so I'd head off with him on a Sunday with our dogs, chasing rabbits through the nearby fields and up into the Burren – a hop, skip and a jump away. At first I was not half as brave as he was, and spent most of my time crying or telling him to wait up because we'd be pushing through thick briars and bushes, trying to follow the dogs who could squeeze through the tiniest spaces. Sometimes a group of us would get together and go hunting. Mostly we would catch nothing, as the dogs barking and the great noise we were making warned off the foxes and the rabbits, who promptly disappeared into their burrows to hide. I loved the excitement of being in a crowd, and the constant barking of the dogs was like music to my ears.

When I was older I went hunting with my friend and neighbour John Kearney, God rest his soul. John had about a dozen dogs of all types. Everyone knew John loved dogs, and people would sometimes drop off strange dogs at his house. He always fed them and treated them as his own. John loved horses too: I have three of his horses still – Sally, Bud and Daisy – and I'm very fond of them.

John spent much of his life working in London on the building sites. When he came back home one year he brought with him a few terriers, very good hunting dogs. When we went out hunting together we would mainly be looking for badgers and foxes, as the foxes would kill quite a few of the newborn lambs in the spring. The pair of us would walk for miles, hunting over the bogs, the mountainside and the valleys. John was a good age but a better walker than I was. Thanks to him I learnt about fields and corners of the landscape I had lived in all my life that I didn't know existed.

While I began to widen my horizons, the magic of the outside world would occasionally come to visit and offer me an even larger prospect. As a young child, my consuming dream was the circus. I wanted not just to watch the circus, but to be a part of it. The noise, the colour and the lights had me riddled with excitement from start to finish, an excitement that has never left me.

When I was five we went to the circus in Ennistymon. I was fascinated by a fantastic white horse which appeared before the crowd. Perfectly trained, it performed wonderful tricks at the drop of a hat, standing for what seemed an endless time on its hind legs.

The seats inside the marquee were wooden and suspended on ropes. The largest family in the town, with almost twenty children, was sitting in the middle row. I was with my friends on the ground in front of them, watching the show. Suddenly, about halfway into the second half, there was a gigantic crash and bang from the back. Some young blaggards from the neighbourhood had reached into the tent and cut through the ropes holding up the seats, thinking it would be hilarious to watch all the seats collapse. It was not funny at all. People were sent crashing to the ground and several of them suffered broken legs. The contrast of such a horrible turn of events with such a happy start to the evening left me somewhat shocked. Yet it didn't put me off going back again.

A few years later, the circus brought a different kind of drama. During the summers my father and I would take the milk from our cows across to the creamery at about ten-thirty every morning, using a donkey and cart. I kept nagging my father to let me take the milk to the creamery by myself. Through sheer stubbornness and persistence I managed to persuade him to give me permission. As it turned out, after all my bravado and enthusiasm, sure the donkey knew the way better than I did. On that particular day, the circus was moving from Lisdoonvarna to Ennistymon. Imagine my excitement as I spotted the lorries and carts catching me up. They passed me one by one – because my donkey was stubborn *and* slow! The final lorry had two trailers on tow. It was fierce long and as the last of the carriages came by, the one which carried the lions, I knew there was no chance it would get past without knocking into my cart. It was simply too big. My donkey and cart were crushed against a high stone wall, and the axle knocked the door of the lions' cage open.

The first lion bounded out, bouncing off the back of the donkey. Its smell drove the donkey wild: he started braying and braying. The second lion followed into the field, startling a cow and her calves. Realising he had hit my cart, the lorry driver jumped out quick as lightning, carrying a whip, net and gun. The lions, bless them, were obviously not used to being free because they didn't bother going far. The lion tamer managed to get one of them to approach him and it was swiftly recaptured. The other lion was not going to be quite as accommodating and made a run for it. Off the circus men went after her . . . and the news spread round town like quickfire. They did recapture the second lion not long after, and no one was hurt except for one cow that had had a leg bitten.

My donkey had been frightened out of its wits, and did not catch its breath back till long after dark that day. The smell of those lions will always stay with me – and with the donkey and all. As compensation for the scare I was given free passes to the circus and a tour round before the next show began. That was the best thing ever, and as I went to sleep that night I knew that my life would not, could not, just include farming.

Intrigue and magic are part of the way of life in the west of Ireland. After all, this is the land of spirits and fairies lurking in the streams, the trees and the bogs, a land of screeching banshees, industrious leprechauns and mischievous pookas, of old grey men, of the Fir Bolg, the legendary ancient rulers of Ireland, and of the ghosts of the children who never got baptised.

Growing up in our seventeenth-century farmhouse was

scary. While I always liked the house during the bright days, I would feel uneasy come the winter nights when friends of my father would come to visit and start talking about fairies and ghosts. These old men told their stories by the light of a candle or a weak oil lamp, which added to the mystery of it all and terrified us youngsters. In their funny voices they would recount tales of beautiful, mysterious women with braided hair down to their waist and long dresses appearing in front of them and shooting straight up into the sky. This, they said, took place at a bush at the crossroads which we had to pass every day. There were stories about wonderful gaiety on moonlit nights when barefooted women holding tiny babies to their breast floated across the surrounding fields lit by every colour of the rainbow, while strange-looking little men played fantastical football matches for hours on end using bushes of furze as their goals.

We also had a haunted house nearby, just a little way down the hill, a long low house with deserted rooms and ravens and crows cawing as they circled the tall trees which surrounded it. Those who dared go into the house heard doors opening all night and tables and chairs moving around when no one was about. Much of my early life was spent trying not to pass this house by night. If I ever had to, I would be sweating and I'd run like hell.

Not surprisingly, most people hereabouts are superstitious. Whenever I see a couple of magpies I'll bless myself two or three times to be safe. And there are many superstitions about love and romance. Crazy stories about potions that will guarantee that someone's affections will be returned – the ashes of a girl's hair or the threads of her shawl mixed into an unsuspecting young man's tea. I have even heard tales of strange concoctions made from frogs' bones or cats' livers.

A small drop of matchmaker's advice

♡ I am a great believer in the magic of romance, that wonderful moment when, often out of nowhere (or so it seems), the first hint of love emerges. What keeps me busy matchmaking is the hope of watching that magical process happen yet one more time. You need to leave space for possibilities: romance is not something that can be calculated, or programmed, or brewed up in a teacup. And even if I thought those infusions and philtres worked, I couldn't recommend them. They'd put a good matchmaker out of a job. ♡

One recent September evening, the festival at Lisdoonvarna was slowly starting to kick in. Johnny, the barman at the Matchmaker pub, who's been there for as long as myself, said, 'Willie, are you ever going to retire?'

Half in jest, I said, 'There's a lot of unfinished work to be done.'

21

He laughed and replied, 'Maybe this time you'll find me a wife.'

'This is your year,' I assured him.

I carried on setting up my stall, the table, chairs, matchmaking book, pen, pint of Guinness, all the essential equipment for the night ahead.

I was just sitting down when I noticed four people with a dog in tow coming directly towards me. They introduced themselves to me as a father and mother, their son Philip and the father's sister. All of them were dressed smartly in grey suits and outfits. They looked serious, with a mission in mind. The aunt was the spokesman for them. She said they were the Murphys. I smiled to myself, saying, So are half of Ireland. She then told me it was my own father who had introduced the couple, Albert and Molly. They had nine children. 'And Philip here will get the land,' she added. I looked at them with more interest. The aunt was about to say more when Philip interrupted.

'Your grandfather made a match for my grandfather and grandmother as well. Will you get me a wife?'

Quickly his mother cut in: 'Philip, your Aunt Maggie will do the talking.' Philip stopped short.

Maggie turned her attention to Philip, quickly explaining how a bull on the family farm had nearly killed him about five years earlier – he had a number of bad scars on his face from the incident – and then looked down at the collie dog that had come in with them and said that it was the dog that had saved his life. The collie, sitting near Philip, wagged his tail and whined a little. I felt he knew we were talking of him. I asked the family to sit down.

Maggie asked me, 'Now Willie, how does this work? Have you anyone in mind for Philip?' At that moment five girls burst laughing into my 'office', one in a raised voice saying, 'Come on, Willie, find a husband for Eileen here,' and Eileen shouting, 'She wants one as well!' Philip seemed fascinated by them all. Maggie quickly moved closer to Eileen, telling her about Philip. She even gave a demonstration of how the bull had attacked him. While the girls were very polite, I felt the aunt had scared them off a little with her over-eagerness. They were young and out for fun and they disappeared with the same laughter they had come in with.

As I looked at the Murphys I said to myself, This won't be too easy. But I felt I had to help them. I was wondering how to approach this. For a moment I thought of my grandfather and father arranging the matches for two generations of the family. Philip's father would not be walking about if it hadn't been for my grandfather, and Philip would not be here but for my father. I had to succeed.

As the evening progressed many people came in and out of my office, and the place grew very busy. The Murphys were leaving and I suggested that they head to the Irish Arms or the Roadside Tavern. Shortly afterwards Philip and his dog arrived back, saying he had been stopped at the door because the dog was not allowed into the pubs. I said, 'Well, you're both welcome here.' Philip seemed a different man without the presence of the older generation. His dog was lovely and getting a lot of admiration, though Philip wasn't doing quite as well.

I was about to close up. It had been a busy night of comings and goings, and lots of drinking going on. Two girls came in and asked if they could join the matchmaking. I said, 'Of course, come and sit down with me.' As they walked around to join me at the table, Philip's dog yelped. One of the girls had stood on his paw. She apologised profoundly to Philip. And as she sat down she stood on the dog's tail. We all laughed, and Philip insisted it was nothing. 'He's grand,' he said. The girl's name was Anna May, and the dog had forgiven her, as he put his head on her lap. She sat stroking the dog's head, all the while chatting away to Philip. Anna May was clearly in the dog's good books. Philip seemed quite relaxed talking to her and Anna May didn't seem perturbed by Philip's scars. As I watched I thought, If this works it will be marvellous. Anna May dragged Philip out for a dance. His dog seemed bemused by this, but happily headed for the dance floor as well.

As the night progressed I informed Anna May that Philip was looking for a partner to marry. She said, 'He seems a lovely person – so gentle,' and I said, 'He is.' I talked to Philip, who was more than pleased. We had made the match, and less than six months later I was invited to Philip and Anna May's wedding. They both looked extremely happy –

for me it was a big achievement. I'm sure if my father and grandfather had been present they would have been just as happy. As they took the wedding photos, I looked down at the dog standing proudly next to the couple. I had to admire him. Not only had he saved Philip's life when he was attacked by the bull, but he had also been an instigator in his marriage. Magic can happen.

2
Plucking the Gander

I was fifteen years old or thereabouts when I made my first match. I had been working out on the Lisdoonvarna road with the bog-cutters – chopping the banks of turf, helping the men by pushing the barrow, taking the turf away and throwing the pieces out to let them dry.

The work was awful hard, and you'd not have any enjoyment doing it on your own, so this other lad, who was five or six years older than me, came down to share the load. We got to talking, and it turned out this fella – Tom Kenny was his name – was stone-mad about the daughter of a farmer nearby. She lived alone with her father – her mother had died a while before – and it was easy enough to see why Tom was crazy about her. She was about sixteen, a beautiful girl, lovely black hair and red cheeks, very good-looking. He was always on about this girl, Bridget, and asking me how he could get to meet her, because she never left the house.

The only regular social scene at that time – and remember this was Ireland in the 1950s – was at Mass. If you wanted to see a girl, you had to watch out for her at Holy Communion. So Tom would turn up to Mass, go up and come back from taking Communion, and as he passed by where the girl was sitting with her father he'd dart a quick look into her seat, and as she stood up for her turn she would be pure red in the face. From my seat a few rows back I used to notice that myself, even though I was still only a kid.

It happened that I heard that the girl's father had a fat pig for sale, so I said to Tom, 'Why don't we go up to the house and pretend to buy the pig?' – even though we had not a penny between us.

We walked across to the farmhouse and knocked on the door. The farmer came out. 'What d'you want?' he grunted. He was a big, tall man and very brusque, and I was a shy kid, almost as shy as Tom. So I hid myself behind Tom a little bit, and said, 'I think you have a big, fat pig for sale.'

'I have,' says he. 'He's over there in the cabin.'

And so we headed over to the pigsty to have a look. We happily squeezed into the sty, and we'd only been in there a couple of minutes when who should come along to join us but young Bridget.

Your man Tom was leaving his hand down on the pig's

back, feeling the fat. 'He's soft,' he said, 'he's not been well fed,' trying to bring the value of the pig down a bit.

Bridget left her hand down on the pig as well. 'That pig is not soft,' she said. 'He was well fed, with barley and milk and cabbage cut up.'

And while they both had their hands down on the pig Tom looked up into her eyes and said, 'Will you ate the pig with me?' – that was the phrase that sticks in my mind, as we often used to say 'ate' instead of 'eat': 'Go in and ate your dinner.' I was surprised because I didn't think he'd have had the nerve. Well, with that, Bridget said nothing but ran off and straight back into the farmhouse and we didn't see any more of her.

About four or five days later her father cycled down to our farm and came into our yard. I was out front fixing something on the jaunting car. And I thought to myself, Jesus, don't tell me he's going to give us the pig, because Tom and I had offered some ridiculously tiny amount of money – since, of course, we didn't really want to buy the animal. It was the last thing we wanted. Up he came and sat himself beside me, on the wall at the front of our house.

'That man,' he said, 'that boy you had with you the other night. He's a nice fella.'

'He is,' I agreed, and I was still wondering what angle he was getting at.

'That fella is a good worker. I'm getting a bit old myself,' he continued, 'and Bridget will be on the farm all on her own. She'd want someone to help look after the place. So has your man any notion of settling down and getting married?'

I was taken aback by this approach, so I had to think quickly. I didn't say that Tom had any such notion, but equally I didn't say he hadn't . . . I said I'd find out.

Off I went to Tom and told him what the farmer had asked me. God, he was delighted, and not long afterwards Tom and Bridget were married – I was invited along, of course – and had a good few children together.

So that was my first match, and I was barely fifteen. It had been something of an accident, but I guess I must have inherited something from my father and his father – the understanding of how to help love come about by steering it in the right direction. I would not be doing what I do without the experience and the instincts they handed down.

Right now I am sitting at the kitchen table in my house in Ballingaddy. Through the window looking south I can see a flock of high clouds drifting in from the sea. On a hilltop across the way is the silhouette of a ruined ring fort that has stood there since long, long before there were Dalys in this valley.

This is a typical Irish cottage kitchen, the teapot permanently on the go, an oilcloth spread over the table. On the wall behind me is the painting of Christ on the cross that my mother left me when she passed away. A photograph of my parents with me as a baby looks down from one of the windowsills. In the hallway is a faded portrait of JFK and Jackie, which used to hang in the old house. From the front room I can hear one of my sons stoking the turf on the fire, which is giving off that warm, pleasant aroma that always makes me feel good, like the smell of coffee brewing or fresh bread baking.

Open on the table in front of me is the book my grand-father and father kept of all the potential matches they ever made – a thick ledger of ruled pages, bound in faded brown boards with a cloth tie to hold it together, bursting as it is with notes and letters and messages. Three lifetimes' worth of pleas for love, requests for romance, and matchmakers' notes.

I still use the ledger, even though it's grown so old that I have to be careful turning over the pages. The book once got left out in the rain by mistake but somehow managed to survive that soaking. It's holding up pretty well, considering. When I opened the book again just now, I found I'd left a little penny whistle tucked inside its pages. The old whistle still played a great tune. I chose a reel I like to play whenever I meet up with the musicians gathering at Cooley's House in Ennistymon or over at O'Connor's pub in Doolin. The story goes that this particular tune was written about a fortnight or so into a honeymoon. A fella and his bride had got married, and he'd brought her back to his family farm. It was the girl's mother-in-law herself who wrote the tune and called it 'Mary, Cut Your Toenails Or You'll Tear the Sheets'! A pretty romantic welcome for the poor girl . . .

This kitchen and this table are at the very heart of my life as a matchmaker. All hours of the day people are dropping by to be fortified by a brew of tea and a chat, and every morning another flurry of letters arrives, asking me to help them find a wife or husband. The phone rings more than you can imagine. Questions, queries, connections, suggestions: the raw material out of which I try to make a match. As a matchmaker you need an open mind and an open door, all year round.

It has always been like this. The kitchen in our old house was the centre of all the matchmaking that went on. People would walk or cycle miles across country to come and see my father, and my grandfather before him. And so, around the table, the discussions and negotiations would carry on through the day and into the night.

During the winter months my father and his friends would gather round the hearth, the only source of heat in the whole house, the best place to fend off the chill. Outside the night would fall hard as nails and black as the smuts from a coal fire. That was why we always preferred to use turf on the fire. The beauty of turf was how bright and clean it was, and the ashes were pure white.

There these old fellas would sit, each puffing on his pipe, many using clay pipes, which were very fragile. From time to time the pipe stems would snap off, and my father might lend them one of his, and perhaps some of his tobacco. He himself had a fine black pipe with a wooden bowl. I remember one man among the group who was a great spitter; he probably had no teeth left, but could chew on some tobacco, then spit the wad ten feet across the room to land it plumb in the middle of the fire. I was always impressed by that.

They would start off playing cards. They'd play for geese, they'd play for hens, they'd play for cigarettes: my father was always quite interested in gambling. When the game was over, and to the accompaniment of the crackling of the wood and the burning of the peat, the men used to spend the rest of the evening tracing family connections, remembering long-dead friends and relatives, working out who was related to who. One of the men always used 'the Big Wind' as a marker for when anything had happened, a terrific gale that had blasted its way across the countryside thirty-odd years before. He'd always say, 'Ah, when my Aunt Maggie married Francis O'Donovan, 'twas five years after the Night of the Big Wind.' Sadly they none of them ever wrote any of these memories down, but I can still recall many of the tales they used to tell of times past, and the stories they told me about my own grandfather.

Alas, I never knew my grandfather, my namesake William Daly. People do say I have something of his looks about me, though. He was a tall man with a distinctive blackish beard, as I had in my younger years before the first streaks of grey crept in.

At the beginning of the last century, when matchmaking was still the most common way for people to meet, William was a familiar figure at all the local cattle fairs and markets, and something of a regular fixture in the pubs afterwards, as he had a fearsome fondness for drink. But he always managed to keep a remarkably clear head when it came to the business of pairing off potential couples, and virtually every family in the area sought his advice at some time or other.

My grandmother was descended from a notorious English soldier, a General Ireton, and brought to the marriage a dowry of a thousand pounds, which was an awful lot of money 130 years ago. I believe she was older than my grandfather and somewhat subdued in comparison, but she was welcomed with open arms for bringing those thousand pounds into the Daly family, which was money they much needed.

I suspect my grandfather donated a fair proportion of that dowry to the Guinness Brewery over the years, even though he had many of his drinks bought for him. People knew that he would usually be in town for the fairs, would track him down to some bar or another and, without making a big song and dance about it, ask for his help and advice, after making sure he was not about to go thirsty. He knew a vast swathe of people, which was why he was so good at matchmaking, and even if he did not know them already, everybody knew William.

Matchmaking was a private matter, though, and people did not enjoy having to discuss such things in public. One of the easiest places to talk about it was at a market, and if my grandfather wasn't in the pub they might find him leaning on the rail of a cattle pen over at the market. The cattle fairs used to open up around five in the morning, so it was an early start, and most of the men would have walked all the way in, so no one had had much sleep the night before.

I remember going to the markets with my father and our own cattle. Nothing much had changed since William's day. The farmers, including ourselves, would bring anywhere from three to ten cattle and we'd take them down into the centre of the town and stand the cows in circles all along the main street, where there were dozens of pubs open from the crack of the day to help keep everyone in good spirits. There's a funny thing about cows: after all the excitement of being walked to the fair, they would usually wait calmly around, no problem, whereas the sheep would be deadly, running all over the place.

The problem with the sheep was that they were all the same colour, and all looked alike, whereas you seldom find an identical cow. To mark our sheep my father would put a little coloured rag on them the day before market day, perhaps an old dress or an apron of my mother's cut up into ribbons and sewn into their wool. 'Twas easier to know them when they were shorn as then we could brand them: our own sheep carried the brand OD, for O Dálaigh, the Irish for Daly.

During the morning of the market my father and I would be standing with our cattle and some stiff old farmer would stroll past – stiff in his attitude, that is, though a nice man – and there'd be a certain amount of banter. He might start poking one of the cows, and there'd be other people watching him, knowing he had unmarried daughters, smiling. But he'd be determined enough to go through with it. 'Now, how much do you want for that cow there, Henry?' And my father would tell him, 'Oh, maybe seven or eight pounds.'

'Ach, you're very high in the price, too high, too dear,' the farmer would say. He would walk around the cow, having another look, and as he came back round would half whisper, almost nonchalantly, 'Now, Henry, could you keep an eye out for somebody for Peggy? She's twenty-two now and sure she'd like to meet a good man.'

That's exactly how it happened in my grandfather's day too. Looking at the cow was just an excuse, of course, and most of the buyers were not really interested in the cows William had brought to the market, but it was a useful way of opening the conversation. You often hear that singles trying to date nowadays find organised events a bit like a 'cattle market'. Well, in Ennistymon and the other local towns, the cattle market was an essential part of the whole business.

My family was not originally from the Ennistymon area. William's branch of the Daly family came from a place called Dysert, a little further inland in the county. He moved over here to Ballingaddy after he married my grandmother, and they used part of her dowry to buy the old house that still stands next door to here. A renowned politician called Charles Lucas had been born in that house, well over two hundred years before I was, in 1713 – he became first a physician and then a Member of Parliament in England. There is even a house named in his honour in Earlscourt Terrace in Dublin. It would be around 1886 or 1887 that William and his wife bought the house off his descendants, and the Dalys are still here, and no intention of leaving any time yet.

My own father left County Clare when he was sixteen or so and headed off to Dublin, where he started off working as a cooper at the Guinness Brewery – appropriately enough, given my grandfather's fondness for the stuff – before taking a job in a pub. Later he opened a B&B, with a bar and restaurant, on Lower Baggot Street in the city, and received a regular supply of guests and honeymooners dispatched to Dublin by my grandfather.

Then my father met and married my mother Kathleen, who had been a nanny for the family of a Dublin judge. A few years later they returned to County Clare, along with my half-brother and sisters – I was not even a twinkle in the old man's eye – and not only took over the running of the family farm but eventually the reins of the matchmaking.

While my father had been away in Dublin the farm had been looked after by a couple of my uncles. My grandfather was never there much of the time: he was far too busy taking care of business at the markets and the fairs and in the pubs, and all of that ate into the time and energy he had available for any farming work. By the time my father and mother were settling into married life, the uncles were getting old and so my father eventually had to come back to help out. He himself was already a good age when I was born, so it was something of a shock to his system to return from the urban life of Dublin and to have to get back into the demands of farming, something he had never had to do since he was a lad.

My mother, who was quite a bit younger than my father, was a country lass who came originally from Galway. But even so she was not at all prepared for what greeted her on the first day they arrived at the farm in Ballingaddy. They had had a long journey right across country from Dublin in a motor taxi, with bags and cases of their clothes and other personal belongings, and must have been absolutely exhausted. My mother stepped out of the taxi, and walked into the kitchen of this seventeenth-century farmhouse, only to find one of my uncles standing there coating the chimney breast with cow dung to stop the soot from the chimney coming into the house.

The surprise, and not least the smell of it, was almost too much for her to bear. She fled straight out of the door, only to see the taxi just disappearing out of sight 150 yards up the lane. I think if the driver had still been there she'd have jumped in beside him and asked him to drive her all the way straight back to Dublin, and I would never have been born . . .

It was normal practice, especially in a farm that had been lived in only by men for so long, to put cow dung on the walls and then paste some whitewash over it. The uncles probably thought they were doing a grand job of decorating the place for her! The problem was that, with the slow postal service and no phones, the uncles had had no idea when exactly my mother and father were turning up. She managed to survive the shock, I'm glad to say.

I don't think my father was that thrilled to have to take over the farm. He never said he didn't want to, but I could tell without him having to say it out loud. In fact he ran the farm quite effectively, but he was feeling his age even as he arrived in the valley. Back then there were only horses to pull the ploughs. It was hard, physically demanding work.

To help out he used to get in a man from over the road, a good man and a great character called Willo who lived in a house over on the top of the hill. Willo would ride over on an ass to come and assist my father as a farm labourer. Now Willo's house was very cold, but we'd have a great fire here, so he'd gladly spend the night at our house. Out we'd go to check the cows by candlelight when they were about to calve. When a cow is ready, you can feel a set of small bones near the tail – the *loigín*, they're called in Irish – drop down, but you have to know where to feel. Willo was clever enough to know that my father was not that knowledgeable about the cows.

'What do you think, Willo?' my father would ask.

'Ach, God damn it,' Willo would say, pulling at his

moustache, ''tis a long night till morning, Henry.' In other words, anything could happen.

'Shall you stay the night, then?' my father would ask.

Willo would settle down by the turf fire, fast asleep and happy and snug in the warm. And oftentimes he would still be asleep when the cow gave birth, all by herself.

I've been known to use Willo's trick myself, once in a while. If I ever want to get out early from a meeting with people from the town, I say, 'Lads, lads, I have to leave now. I have a cow calving.' They are always very helpful, 'Oh God, Willie, you go on away.' It works wonders – townspeople think a calf has to be treated like a baby. Most country folk don't fall for it though, and just say, 'Can't the cow calve on her own?' I was involved in a committee for a festival once, and I used this excuse so many times some old fella finally said to me, 'Jesus, Willie, how many cows have you got?!'

Although my father never felt that comfortable with the farming obligations, the matchmaking seemed to sit more easily with him. He was already familiar with many of the people roundabouts, having been born on the farm. So he knew how to suggest that this one or that one might marry someone he had in mind. But his personality was completely different from my grandfather's.

He had a good stocky build, and always wore a hat. People used to tell me, 'James Cagney is awful like your father to look at!' He was a very quiet, shy man, not at all outgoing like my grandfather, which was something of a disadvantage because so much time had to be spent talking to people at fairs, or funerals or weddings – any kind of social gathering. And he was never fond of the drink. He was not a teetotaller but very measured in his drinking. He'd have one or two but that would be it. He was always warning me about the danger of drink, because he had seen the damage it had done to other people. 'I've seen too much of the outcome of that,' he'd tell me.

In the pub at cattle fairs, I noticed when he tried to discreetly throw a drink someone had bought him into the fire. And I also observed fellas looking at him and whispering to each other, as much as to say, 'Well, who is he, who'd waste the present of a drink?' And even laughing at him for it. You see, many times at the fairs people would get very drunk all right. It would be their big day out, and some of them feeling loaded with the money from selling the cattle would have spent it by the end of the day. But careful men like my father knew the cattle money was all they had, and that it had to last a long time to pay the bills.

In this attitude he was a typical Daly. They were all extremely strait-laced, terribly diligent. Their life was their work. My father's very quietness, though this meant he was less at ease in big social settings, was none the less an asset, as he possessed a judgement and an integrity that everyone admired.

What you have to understand is that at the time, matchmaking was a vital part of the way of life here. So a great discretion was required, because money lay at the root of it all, money not necessarily in the form of cash, but of cattle, sheep, horses and turf. And the quality of the land involved would also be part of the equation.

The setting of the dowry was all a question of balance. If a girl was good-looking then her family were in the fortunate position of never having to pay so much out. But if she was – how shall we put it? – a little less than good-looking, then the money and the assets were critical.

Strangely, making money was not why my father and grandfather were matchmakers – and that's still true for me today. Their day-to-day income came from the farm. People were poor and couldn't afford to pay for matchmaking services, so there was never any fee as such, though there might have been a gift after a successful match. I'd say there were almost always a few shillings and drinks for my grandfather. I remember my father being given a load of turf, four horse-drawn trailers of it, and on a couple of occasions getting some old army clothes or some rainwear. And somebody once gave me a ram!

A small drop of matchmaker's advice

♡ *Nothing makes me happier, like most folk, than to see a couple falling in love. I never tire of the romance. But, although there is no longer the same kind of need for negotiating a match in such a practical way as my father and grandfather did, it is still a great idea to keep a level head on you when you're weighing up a love match. Maybe the person you meet is not precisely what you had imagined, but be prepared to look at all the wider aspects of this new relationship, and take those into account as well when you are deciding whether to move things along. However, don't dither too long. Keep in mind that, as my mother told me, long churning makes bad butter.* ♡

The first match I ever witnessed my father make was when I was a young lad of ten or eleven. I had walked to a nearby house through the fields with my father, who was taking me to the 'plucking of the gander', as it was known. This was the serious part of the matchmaking process, the negotiations held between the prospective bride and groom to determine what each was bringing to the marriage. But that evening I had no idea what the 'plucking of the gander' meant. I knew we always had a goose at Christmas and thought it might be something to do with that. My only apprehension was about our walk through the night. As the flickering oil lamp my father was carrying lit up the trees and bushes, all those stories I had heard of ghosts and spirits living in them gave me goosebumps.

We found the family gathered in the parlour, the room generally reserved for formal get-togethers around Christmastime. On this particular evening the parlour had been cleared and fastidiously cleaned for the important matter at hand, and a whole gaggle of relatives had turned up to add their weight to proceedings.

One of the daughters of the house, Catrin, was a gorgeous happy-go-lucky girl, in her late twenties, rosy-cheeked, blue-eyed. Her father had died some time before and so it fell to her aunt and an uncle to handle the arrangements for her marriage.

My father greeted the family and headed into the parlour along with all the adults and the farmer who was keen to secure Catrin's hand in marriage. As a mere boy, I had to stay outside in the kitchen, where Catrin, her sisters and a couple of other young lads were corralled – Catrin was not allowed to be part of the discussion. On some occasions, if the fella who was to be married was also young, he would be excluded from the meeting too, and an older relative would handle the business aspects for him. But in this case the man who was interested in Catrin was in his sixties, and well able to look after his side of the bargain. He had never been married, and had spent most of his life with his mother until she had died a few years previous.

There was added pressure on the negotiations: Catrin's older brother had recently got married, and wanted the aunt and uncle out of the house. So the farmer would be getting not just Catrin, but the uncle and aunt into the bargain.

Compared to the formal, sober mood in the parlour, there was a real party atmosphere in the kitchen. It was an exciting thing when a match was being made and plenty of laughter followed. I remember they had a gramophone and some music playing. I couldn't believe how much mirth there was. Catrin's sisters kept pinching her, teasing her about the prospect of her marriage, whispering little inside jokes to each other and giggling at their own remarks. I sat there, trying not to get in their way but revelling in the mood of anticipation and mystique and their girlish fun, which I thought was wonderful.

Then my father popped his head round the door of the parlour. 'Willie, will you go and get my pipe out of my coat pocket?' His coat was hanging up by the front door, so I nipped over, took the pipe out and went into the parlour to pass it to him. The grown-ups barely noticed I was there, so I took the opportunity to squat silently in a corner and listen to everything that was going on. Normally I would never have been allowed to stay, but they were all so caught up in the conversation, so engrossed in what they were doing, that I knew if I piped down I would get a peek into the mysterious world of adults. And the intricacies of matchmaking.

They were just entering the most crucial part of the negotiations: the amount of the dowry that would go with the girl. As it happened, Catrin's aunt was giving the prospective husband a hard time; she was a seasoned negotiator.

Although there was plenty of land involved – maybe a hundred acres or more – she was claiming that the bulk of his land was worthless, mostly marshy bogs, thereby reasoning that they should not have to pay out so much for Catrin's dowry. But the man was equally tough and holding out for a good sum. He had originally asked for £200, and the family had offered £90 or so in reply. They were prepared to go up to £120, but didn't want to budge above that. He was adamant that was not going to be enough, and said his final offer would be £135, take it or leave it. After a whispered conversation the aunt and uncle agreed with that, and the uncle said that the money would be coming back from America, from some of their family who had made the long journey over.

Eventually the niceties of the deal were concluded, and off the aunt went to break the news to Catrin. She cut her aunt's explanations off short. 'Oh, I don't give a straw about the arrangements,' she said with a merry smile – she really didn't care at all, and was quite happy to go along with things. I remember one of her sisters asked her if she was not scared of marrying a man who was so much older, to which she replied, 'No, not at all.' She was quite fearless, and I've learnt over the years that fearlessness is a very useful attribute when you're about to embark on a relationship! She was, I think, simply happy to be able to set up home with the man, who, though older, was handsome, and she was ready to be a mother. And she knew her aunt and uncle were in a difficult predicament, being forced by her brother to move out of the house, and she was happy to help them out, since she had a kind and generous spirit.

Catrin and the older man did indeed get married, went on to have seven children, and both lived to a right good age. The husband must have been nigh on ninety-seven when he died, and Catrin reached an equally venerable age. So the very first match I ever saw was a very successful one.

A small drop of matchmaker's advice

♡ People always ask me how I do what I do. What's the secret? It's hard to explain in words exactly. There's not an exact recipe or method. It's a mixture of intuition and an ability to move things forward in a subtle manner. I personally use gentle little nudges, a touch of encouragement, and I think I know how to create the right atmosphere. I do feel that I, like my father and grandfather, have an insight into the shifting tides and seasons of human nature, but you also have to be prepared to deal with the unpredictable. If we knew exactly how love would go, life would be far too dull. You cannot control love, you can only try to help guide it – and I think that's what a good matchmaker does. ♡

Once a 'plucking of the gander' was over and the match successfully made, there would be a marvellous mood in the house, great gaiety and excitement, and one almighty hooley. Often as not, a bunch of musicians would turn up to play. From nowhere trays of buns and jam would appear, and although there would be a certain amount of drink to hand, they'd have plenty of pots of tea at first, so the party might start off slow enough.

The men of the family would come out of the room with the groom. All of a sudden the murmuring and the laughter would cease for a little while. It would grow very quiet, as this would often be the future bride and groom's first time of meeting, more or less, and certainly the first time since they both knew they were definitely going to be married.

With the formal introduction out of the way, everyone could relax. The girl would be standing there, tossing her hair, awful pleased. Either she was marrying the fella that she liked, and that would be fantastic, or if the match was a compromise, within reason it would be fine, because in these days past getting her own home meant so much to her. And now the shenanigans could begin in earnest.

Going with my father to the plucking of the gander, and wandering round the festivities afterwards with my eyes and ears wide open, this was my informal education in the ways of matchmaking.

Going to school seemed somehow less magical by contrast, although getting there was often great fun. When I was five and just starting out at the local school, I'd be tagging along each morning with my sister Delia and another large family of children from further down the road who used two black asses, both very good-natured, as their mode of transport. All the older girls were mad about me, as the newest kid on the block, and they'd swing me up to sit on the ass in the middle of a crowd of them, five or six of us on each donkey. Then the bigger lads would create a bit of mischief by bating the animals, prodding them with a pin, so the asses would suddenly start and all of us on board would fall off, landing in a laughing heap.

Because my family had connections to business in Dublin, where my aunts and uncles worked, us young ones on the farm would occasionally be sent parcels with quality clothing. My mother was always smartly turned out. There was one day when my parents came to school, which was not often, when I was maybe six, and I remember thinking, Jesus, my mother is very smart and good-looking. She was well dressed, wearing a fur coat and the kind of clothes that a lot of other country people never had.

Now when we received one package which contained some new clothes for us, that we didn't mind, but there were also leather shoes, and that was a potential embarrassment, as this would mean we would be the only children in the parish to have a pair. It sounds unbelievable now, but none of the other children had shoes, not even in the winter – their feet were always black with dirt and blue with cold, and covered with bruises and cuts from walking to school. So my older sister Elizabeth devised a great plan. Each day we would leave the house, waving goodbye to Mother while wearing our new shoes. And then, as soon as we were out of sight off the shoes would come, and we'd hide them in the ditch so we could put them back on when we returned from school later that day.

Everything went well for the first two weeks. Then one day it rained and rained. My mother decided to meet us on the way with a few coats to keep us dry. It didn't take her long to notice our bare feet. Well, nobody messed with my mother and it was no good pretending that somehow we had all lost our shoes along the way. She had all the information out of us in seconds, and of course there was hell to pay.

There was plenty of discipline at the school, Gortown National School, built in 1893, three miles away over the crossroads and straight on. The buildings are still standing, and whenever I drive past I flash straight back to my time inside the classroom. Oh, those teachers were strict, and the principal teacher in particular was a devil with a stick. He once put out a bone in my sister Elizabeth's wrist that was never the same again. Yet at the time, it was all accepted; the teacher prior to him had been awful strict too. It was the way it was done. You just had to stick it out.

There were also stand-up fights after school. I never enjoyed the fighting, but you wouldn't be given a choice; you had to join in. There was one big family of kids, nine or ten of them, from over on the other side of the lake. We had no real animosity between us, but at seven or eight years old we would just get together and fight, this side of the lake against the other, for no real reason other than letting off energy.

When I was in the Infants, I would have to walk back from school on my own, as we were let off one hour earlier than the rest of the kids. The journey was the best part of an hour's walk, and I had to do it in all weathers, along a rough old road full of potholes and flints and stones that would try hard to stub your bare feet and give you mighty bruises. From time to time I'd cross paths with one man, dressed in black, with a hat and a stick for the cattle. He never once spoke to me, but he'd use his stick and pretend it was a gun to shoot me. And sometimes I'd meet a small man riding on an old white horse. He was quite elegant, though he had no saddle, riding up from town with a message. I was pretty shy at the time. 'What o'clock is it, sonny?' he'd ask me. I would never answer. They were both quite frightening for a small boy, and I'd end up running most of the way home.

One adult I did feel comfortable with was Willo, the labourer who helped my father out on the farm. He and his brother Jonno were always nice to me. 'How are you getting on, Willie?' they'd ask, and maybe give me a bull's-eye or a cheap white sweet. I was very fond of sweets but these white sweets were not easy to eat. Willo had had an accident with his leg and often had some sacking wrapped round it. So this sweet emerged from his pocket covered with sacking and hayseeds. I'd have to decide whether to eat the sweet then and there, or take it home, wash it and carefully pick all the seeds out. But still, a sweet was a sweet, and we would almost never have a sweet.

If I saw Willo on my way home and he was coming my way he would bring me and my bag up on his donkey, which was a great relief, and we'd drop by his house, the little thatched house at the top of the hill. I'd sit down with Willo and we'd talk over a cup of tea. I was very fond of Willo. He had a beautiful black and white pony on his farm, and he always used to say to me, 'Willie, I'll leave you that pony yet, I'll give him to you one day,' though I don't suppose he really meant it. He knew how much I loved horses.

In the evening he would often walk over to our house with me to listen to my father's radio. My family was one of the few in the area with a wireless radio, a lovely large piece of furniture made of brown wood with a cloth front over the speaker and half a dozen good-sized knobs. The radio was operated by one wet and one dry battery. The wet battery was ten inches by three and a half square and made of heavy glass, and needed to be recharged every ten days or so. My father would take the battery in the ass and cart down to Gilla Skerret's garage. He always told us kids not to touch it as the acid would burn our hands. The dry battery was very colourful, three inches high and one foot square.

We got the best reception at Christmas as my parents would make it a priority to have both of the batteries in good nick, but even so the good reception was short-lived as most times either the dry or the wet would quickly start losing power and the volume would go very low. You would have to have your ear close to it to hear it properly. During the Second World War my father would try to listen to the news each night. Our neighbours knew this and would regularly ask him, 'How is the war going, Henry?' so he could relay any news to them.

The radio was kept in the parlour, a room which was not used a lot, small but quaint with nice ornaments, carpet, the best furniture in the house and the radio in pride of place. Just before ten o'clock in the evening my father and any neighbours who had come over to play cards would look at their watches and say, 'We'll go and listen to the news.' At this point Willo would announce, 'God damn it, Henry, we'll go up and see what Shoeman has to say' – he meant Harry Truman, President of the United States. And they would all troop into the parlour. Sometimes the men would get annoyed as the radio would only last a minute or two before dying out.

My father told me that, towards the end of the war, one other house in Ennistymon had a wireless radio and again quite a number of people would be there listening to the news, especially as most families would have a relative in the UK or America.

The news came over the radio that the Japanese had invaded Pearl Harbor, but the signal was so weak that someone listening to the radio in Ennistymon misheard and thought it was Bellharbour that had been attacked. Bellharbour was a quayside village about fifteen miles north of Ennistymon. The news that Bellharbour had been attacked spread quickly and an alert call went out through the town. Men gathered to see what was the best strategy to adopt, and it was assumed that Ennistymon, being the biggest town, would be the next to be attacked; there was panic and pandemonium. They agreed that the local delivery-man Micko Nestor should block the entrance to the town by dumping cartloads of stones and rocks. They blockaded the road opposite the Protestant church as it had high walls. They vigorously worked at this and armed with spades, forks and shovels bravely waited for the imminent onslaught by the Japanese Army.

My father was going into town the following morning, and when he reached the barricade he was told what was happening. He informed the men that he had also listened to the radio the night before and that it wasn't Bellharbour the Japs had attacked but Pearl Harbor. He said you never saw such relief on men's faces.

This was my world as a boy, living on the farm, sometimes helping my mother and father out with the cows, trudging off to school, trying to dodge the teacher's stick, listening to Willo's stories over tea and biding my time, waiting for the next stage of my life to begin, because I knew I wanted to move on to something different.

It was as though I was waiting to move out of winter and into the spring. Winter was always a difficult time for me, a very threatening season, and the long, long dark evenings would start soon after the end of August. I felt this particularly when I was in my mid-teens and going out a lot. We had no TV, electricity or running water other than the pelting of the rain on the roof. I was sometimes restless and bored and working very hard with the cows, sheep and horses. I loved where I lived, but I missed what I imagined as the city lights and city life, fuelled by the stories I heard about dances in London, in Cricklewood or Hammersmith, from neighbours who had been over to England.

Even when I got older and returned from a city break to alight from the bus at Kellys Cross, as I took that first step out of the bright lights of the bus into total darkness and the strong breeze from the Atlantic and set off home to an oil lamp or candle, I felt as though I were stepping back in time to an ancient and gloomy age. It would take me a little while to adjust back to rural life.

Many was the time, when I was younger, that I would say as we reached the darkest nights of November and December, 'I'm going to die, Jesus, literally die. I'll never survive this.' The minute spring came in, bang, I'd be off like a shot. Spring and summer are my times.

3
Changing Fortunes

When I was still in my teens I started telling fortunes during the Matchmaking Festival in Lisdoonvarna, reading people's palms in the pubs and using a healthy dose of blarney to entertain the crowds. If I ever ran out of money and I needed some way of putting a few extra pounds in my pocket, it fitted the bill perfectly. All the women at the festival wanted to know when they'd get married and how many children they'd have. There wouldn't be much light in the dark corners of the pubs, so I'd use matches to throw a little light on their hands to add to the overall drama. I was simply messing, to be honest, but as sure as Jesus it often turned out true. I couldn't believe it.

One time these six women were in town for a Saturday night, and I was over in Lynch's Hotel. They kept saying, 'Read our fortunes, Willie,' and I'd be saying, 'No, I can't,

I have to be somewhere else. In fact I should have been there about an hour ago, I'm awful late.' But then they cornered me so I couldn't escape and said, 'Just do the fortune for one out of us then,' and I couldn't really say no. A big crowd had gathered around, and I got my box of matches out. The woman whose palm they wanted me to read was considerably older than the rest of the group, so I agreed to tell her fortune.

'When is she getting married?' was, as I knew it would be, the first question one of her friends asked. 'This woman is already married,' I said, which turned out to be true, a pretty shrewd guess after all, and everybody let out a roar. Then of course the next question was 'How many children has she?' Well, it's awful easy to tell someone how many children they're going to have, because no one can argue with you, but this question was a real stickler.

I got my matches out again to give myself a little more time to think. Now, the women had a fellow with them who came from Lisdoonvarna, a great character and a good friend of mine called John Petty. We were all in a cluster, and he had his arm around me and his hand on my shoulder. 'How many children has she got, Willie?' they asked again. The next thing I know John gave me eight taps on the shoulder. So you can imagine when I mentioned the figure eight, the Lord save us, I had to run, I literally had to run.

At this point in my life, when I was eighteen or nineteen, I was not planning to be a matchmaker at all. With the matchmaking so much a part of my family's life, you might have thought it was inevitable I would in turn become a matchmaker in my father's and grandfather's footsteps. Perhaps Fate always decreed that I would do just that, but for many long years it never entered my mind. Indeed there was a point in my young life, when I was twelve or thirteen, when I seriously considered joining the priesthood. Now that, I can assure you, is one confession that would amaze even my closest acquaintances.

Our local church was over at Kilshanny: you can see the church just across the fields from behind this house. My family was never particularly religious, although we went to Mass there once a week, and like everyone else we would know and observe the festivals and be aware of the round of holy days and saints' days that marked the cycle of the seasons. Every year I still look forward to celebrating St Brigid's Day on 1 February, the traditional beginning of spring in Ireland.

The rosary would be said in our house most nights; my father would get down on his knees to recite it at around ten o'clock. During my teenage years in the 1950s there was a movement to encourage people back to praying regularly, called the Prayer Crusade, led by Father Peyton, a priest from County Mayo. 'The family that prays together stays together' was his message, and he marched with his followers around Ireland, and overseas, to spread the word.

One summer, in 1955, the crusade was touring the

country and we learnt that they would be marching down from Lisdoonvarna to Ennistymon. The whole of my school went up to Kellys Cross to join in the crusade. The day was beautiful and sunny, and the tar was melting – the old dirt road had finally been tarred over about a year or less before. It was real hot, so hot that the tar was sticking to my bare feet. We stood waiting a good while for Father Peyton to join us, jumping from one foot to another but afraid to move in case we lost our place. Eventually through the shimmer above the road we could see the procession moving and swaying slowly towards us, with the sound of chanting hanging in the air. Father Peyton led the way, dressed in fine robes that would have graced a bishop, with three other priests alongside him, and perhaps a thousand people behind them, stretching back over half a mile. We joined in as they went past the cross, and the walking was grand. It was a marvellous spectacle which affected us all, and revived the notion of prayer in the locality for a good two or three years afterwards.

Each year a group of Christian Brothers would visit our school. The monks addressed us boys, and the nuns who accompanied them would talk to the bigger girls. These monks painted an attractive, glamorous picture of their work, of the chance to head off around the world to help spread the word of Our Lord, a great thing to do with your life. There would usually be one of the Brothers who'd been a mission-ary out in the Far East and would show us beautiful photographs of his life there. For a while there this notion had a great deal of appeal for me – and two of my good friends, who sat either side of me at school, ended up joining the Brothers.

One of these two fellas, Mickey, and I were thirteen or so when we went out of a night to a festival over at Lisdoon-varna, not the Matchmaking Festival but a *fleadh* for music and general craic. We had got a lift up there from a local man we knew, and as we arrived outside one of the pubs he said, 'Would you lads come in for a drink?' Well, we'd never say no, of course. In we went, and he asked us, 'Will you have a bottle of stout?' so I said we would. We would never have been forward enough to ask for one ourselves.

He brought over a couple of bottles of stout for us. The next thing we saw this awful tall man coming across to us, and we could see a little religious collar around his neck. We quickly hid our bottles out of sight behind us. This priest walked straight over to us and said, 'Boys, now remember, I want you to make sure that you mind your pledge.'

We looked as wide-eyed and innocent as we knew. 'Oh, we will, Father, we will.' He stayed around for a while, looking back over at us to check we were being true to our word, so we kept the bottles down by our side and eventually managed to shuffle a little bit away so he couldn't see us.

We drank a good few bottles enough that night, although I know I wasn't drunk and I'd say my friend wasn't, even if he was merry enough. Mickey was the kind of young fella who, when he started getting the taste of drink, might well have gone over to a table and taken more drink off it as well.

The following day I was meant to be working with him a few miles away, but he never appeared. The following two days he didn't show up either, so on the fourth day I said to a cousin of his there, 'Where's Mickey?' And the cousin told me what had happened. The night when we had been out drinking Mickey had gone back home and his parents had found the smell of drink on him. They were so strict that they decided he should go off and join the Christian Brothers the very next day. That's something, isn't it? A Christian Brother at thirteen. And I would think he had a difficult time, because he was always a wild kind of a lad. The thought of it put me off the priesthood once and for all.

I am still a little religious, though, and even if I do not go to church as regularly as I once did, I rarely let a week pass without going into a church wherever I am. I like to go in to light a candle and say a couple of prayers for those that would be dead.

I suspect I would not have made a very good priest – in fact I'm sure I wouldn't have – but part of being a match-maker is being an extremely good listener; and I have heard stories and problems told to me in confidence that would have rocked any confession box. I try hard never to make hasty judgements about what I hear, or about these people who have come to me in hope or despair, but I do find myself tuning in to what I suppose you could say was their spiritual side. It's not quite as religious an experience as that sounds, but in matchmaking there has to be some connection that works at a very instinctive level.

I was no longer tempted by becoming a priest, but I had to grow up and take on adult responsibilities earlier than most of my friends. My father had turned seventy before I was ten, and even with outside help he was growing older and stiffer, and finding it more and more difficult to handle the business of working our farm.

My half-brother Michael had helped a good bit on the farm, but he left for England when I was eleven. Although he came back on holiday for a year or two, and helped to cut the turf, he then decided to stay over there for a good while, ten or eleven years. My sisters had gone to school in Dublin. It was awful lonely without them all. So I was no more than thirteen years old when I started taking over a lot of my father's duties.

I found myself doing things at thirteen that hardly any other fella my age would know: going off alone to all the fairs, buying and selling cattle, looking after our farm's finances. If other lads went to the fairs they'd be there with their father or an uncle, who'd be in charge of paying out any money. The cattle dealers were tough and awful mean, and I had to learn to negotiate with them, handle money, think about turning a profit, and generally keep my wits about me. Things were tight, as when I took over the farm we only had four cows, so there was little money to work with, and less to spare.

The work never got me down, though. In fact I enjoyed it – I was born blessed with a happy disposition, thank the Lord. And the physical activity was fine for a youngster. It kept me healthy and I've carried on working like that all my life. This all made me feel very grown-up, doing a man's work.

Of course it took a toll on my schooling. I missed a lot of days, and then stopped, but to be truthful, I was happy to leave school. I did spend a year each at a monastery school and a technical college, but to make up for some of what I had missed I took night classes in carpentry, which I enjoyed, making chairs, wheelbarrows, ladders and horse cars.

After my brief flirtation with the priesthood, there was a period at fourteen when I fancied becoming a soldier, by signing up for the FCA, An Fórsa Cosanta Áitiúil, which was the reserve defence force. It was like a wave, all my friends were joining. I decided to enlist on the quiet, not to tell my parents as it would worry them. I went to a hall in Lahinch to enrol late that January. It was a hive of activity. The hall had a timber floor and everyone was wearing hobnailed boots. All I could hear was 'Clé-deas, clé-deas,' 'Left-right, left-right.'

Towards the end of February I was given my uniform: a green cap, jacket with brass buttons, trousers, leather leggings, leather boots and a heavy topcoat. This was so exciting. I couldn't believe I was in the army. On 4 March I got my gun and bayonet, and a couple of weeks later, on St Patrick's Day, we took part in a marching display in Ennistymon. I had hidden my uniform and gun in an old unused cowshed near my house, as I dared not take it home. What I forgot to do, though, was to shine the brass on my cap and uniform. When I arrived I was eaten out of it by the senior army staff. My friends ushered me into Reynolds's little shop nearby, where we bought a tin of Brasso and quickly polished up my buttons and badge. We marched to our town just as Mass was over and we were very proud of ourselves. I joked and said to my friend as we marched along, 'I notice most of us are on the wrong step. God help Ireland!' Several times we tried to change step but we could never get it right.

That night I got drunk and forgot to take off my uniform and hide it with my gun before I went home. My father opened the door, never said a word, and put me into bed, boots and all.

The older lads in the FCA expected us younger ones to behave well and respect the army. After all, they had entrusted us with guns. But one day we got carried away with the whole thing and stopped off in a pub, and then we decided to go off to a dance in a village, seven miles or so away.

On the way I went into a shop to buy some biscuits and an old woman came out to serve me. I must have looked a scary sight with my gun and bayonet and the state of me, because she passed clean out and her son stormed into the shop and ordered us all to get out.

The next time we went to training one of the sergeants approached us and told us to give back the guns and uniforms as they'd found out – alerted by the shopkeeper's son, I think – that we were too young. You had to be seventeen to join the FCA. And that put an abrupt end to my career in the armed forces.

I started going out drinking with a bunch of lads I knew. Oh, we thought we were big men. At that time I was the worst-affected by drink in the company. I would get sick so easy, after a few pints, and stay sick all night and next day. Despite this, whenever I managed to get a little extra money from the fortune-telling or by doing work for other farmers we would head into Ennistymon and get drunk.

A pint of Guinness cost one shilling and threepence. There were twenty shillings in the pound, so we would have been able to squeeze fifteen or sixteen pints of Guinness out of one pound. But no one ever had a whole pound; if we were very lucky one of us might have a ten-shilling note, which was a lovely colourful red note. And most times it would be Tom Skinny who had the ten-shilling note. Tom always had money. As his family only had a small farm, we wondered how he managed it. He always carried his money in an old stocking. Someone said it came from his three old aunts who lived in the farmhouse too, he must have got it from them. They would be receiving the pension and he would be minding the money for them, telling them he'd be getting Masses said for this relative or that ailing family friend, or for them.

They would sure be annoyed if they thought he was drinking it all away!

We would turn up at Vaughan's or Considine's, Cullinan's and McMahon's. Many of the proprietors would only pour us one pint before telling us, 'Now go home and dig a bucket of spuds for your mothers, you're too young.' But some pubs were nicer to us. One of our favourites had a lovely young girl from the country working behind the counter. People used to say she looked just like Audrey Hepburn. On a quiet night there we might have only the price of one pint between us, but she would kindly keep giving us drink. I think she hated being in the bar alone as she was only sixteen or seventeen and she enjoyed our company – but she ran the risk that the older men, when they came in, would give out to her for serving us alcohol.

There was a lovely pub we frequented, which was run by a couple who were both a good age. We knew the husband, Paddy, because he would cut turf with us, so we felt good in his house. His wife Bridie would generally look after the bar in the mornings as her mind used to get tired in the evenings. She liked me because I'd listen to her and take time to talk to her. The other boys just ignored her because they didn't find her interesting.

At some point in the evening Paddy would leave the bar to go out and have his supper and Bridie would come out to greet everyone. No one would answer her, so she'd greet me, saying, 'How are you, Willie, how's your mother, how's your father?' And her lovely innocent expression would change to suit her next statement: 'Isn't the weather just awful, will it ever stop raining?' Being always optimistic I'd say, 'It will, Bridie, it will.' Then she'd smile and agree with me.

Bridie couldn't pour a good pint for the life of her. There was an art to it which she had never mastered. You had to pour a little bit, let it settle, come back, add another drop, three times or more. Bridie would do it too quick, try and pour a pint in the one run, and my friends said her pints made them sick. But since I knew I was going to get sick anyways and in the knowledge that Bridie always got confused about the price of drink during the course of the evening, I felt it a good time to get a round. As our drinks got lower Bridie would notice and ask, 'Are ye all right, boys, will I fill them again?' The boys would say no, they would wait for the husband to come back as they wanted a good pint. I would notice the rejection on her face, and could never resist saying, 'Go on, now, fill them up again, Bridie.' She would start singing, and I'd turn to the boys: 'Wasn't that lovely, lads?'

But the best was to come. If Bridie was terrible at pouring pints, she was worse at adding up and counting out money, especially at the end of a long evening, but it never stopped her trying. With great confidence and after lots of writing numbers down on a piece of paper, crossing them out and starting again, she would eventually arrive at a fairly random amount. And then, whatever money we gave her, she'd always ask us, 'How much have I to give you back as change now?' As a fellow said one day, 'There should be a pub like this in every town.'

A small drop of matchmaker's advice

♡ A pint of Guinness has to be perfectly poured, and it is an art that – like matchmaking – needs a steady hand, plenty of patience and a certain flourish. Only then can you fully appreciate that distinctive flavour and charm. A Guinness is famous for helping embolden the timid, and providing a little extra courage at critical moments. As they say, you can never kiss an Irish girl unexpectedly. You can only kiss her sooner than she thought you would. ♡

One night I was at a dance in the town hall, and a friend and I met two lovely girls. There was a heavy misty fog and we took them for a stroll up Larry's Lane, one of the local courting spots. The old road was narrow and had walls of earth and stone with plenty of grass on top, so there was a certain amount of privacy, since although the lane was close to the town it was not used much in the late evenings as there were no houses up there. Sure and if it was not my first time there with a girl. That same night a local bully-boy we called Bully Broderick had also met a girl. My friend Noel suggested we go to the cowshed along the lane. As we were about to go inside the bully rushed up with his girl, pushed us aside and entered the shed. We could hear loud voices. Scully, a local drunk who had decided to sleep off the excesses of the day's drinking before going home to his wife, was being forcibly evicted out the door by Bully Broderick.

Suddenly a warning whistle rang out from Paddy Sixpence that none other than Father Tom was coming. He was a priest notorious for breaking up courting couples at Larry's Lane, or another place we called 'down the Glen', a quiet little spot full of trees and bushes along by the river at the Falls Hotel. Father Tom was a real devil. He would go on patrol maybe two or three times a night, on the hunt for any moral weakness. He had a big blackthorn stick in his hand and he'd beat anyone he found down there.

At Paddy's whistle, boys and girls scattered, leaping over walls, across ditches and through hedges. Noel, the girls and I ran for cover behind a bush. We could hear the sound of the priest's boots on the gravel and the rustle of his long black robe. Frozen in fear, we all held our breath. He was so close to where we were hiding we could sense his presence. If Father Tom had reached out he could have touched us. He was straining to hear any sound.

Out of the silence came the bully's voice saying, 'I prom-ise you, Mary, I'll be careful.' With that Father Tom gave out a great roar, made a run for the cowshed and there was the thwack of the blackthorn stick, with the bully crying and pleading with Father Tom to stop. The door burst open and the bully came flying out, his trousers down to his ankles, jumping and running as fast as he could get away. Father Tom was lashing his white arse, shouting, 'I'll beat the devil out of you, you blaggard!'

The next Sunday Father Tom vehemently denounced the carry-on in Larry's Lane and delivered a lengthy sermon on morals. We all felt he knew we had been there and was talking directly to us. The bully stood red-faced at the back of the church. It was rumoured he could not sit down again for at least two weeks after the beating.

My first true romance came not long after. It was a fair day in Ennistymon, where I had some horses for sale. Groups of girls would come down the town from the convent, and this lunchtime there were about five of them together, giggling and laughing – oh, they were bold when they were in a group.

I was trying to make a deal with a man for a lovely red and white cob for £20, a lot of money then. We had slapped hands about five times. He was offering me £17, and the schoolgirls were shouting, 'Sell, Willie, sell!' I was a little embarrassed but was happy to see the girls. One of them was staying in the background not saying anything, but she looked like an angel; I heard them call her Tricia.

I eventually sold my horse for £19 and £1 for luck. The new owner and I were talking when the girls grabbed Tricia and flung her in towards us. She grabbed hold of me so as not to fall. She looked divine so I bent down and gave her a little kiss as her friends roared and cheered.

The next fair day couldn't come quick enough, but disappointingly it rained very heavily and I didn't see Tricia: the nuns would not let the girls out in the rain. I had to wait for the next opportunity to see her, a sheep fair. As I looked down the street I wondered whether Tricia and the girls would get through, as the whole town was a blanket of sheep. Lo and behold, at half-twelve I could hear the sound of laughing and fun coming up the street. It was the girls. My heart was thumping with delight – my shyness was quite big at times and I wondered what I would say. At first I could not see Tricia 'midst all the people. The girls caught and lifted up a little lamb I had, white with a black face. Then I saw Tricia fussing about the lamb. I felt so good. Her friends asked, 'Willie, can you come to Corofin Lake on Sunday? We're having a picnic.' I gladly said I would. Again Tricia looked so pretty. I felt so different, I had to be in love.

Come Sunday I cycled out to Corofin, about fifteen miles away. There were nine or ten boys and girls at the lake but no Tricia. After a while her friend told me Tricia's last boyfriend had unexpectedly arrived, and suggested I return for a dance that night. I went back to the farm, milked the cows by hand, fed the calves and got ready to go to the dance with a friend. We joked along the way, him laughing more at me cycling this distance twice in one day. When we arrived there were no signs of the young people at all. Later on an older friend of Tricia's came over and informed me that the girls were not allowed to attend the dance. A little disappointed, we headed back to Ennistymon. I had cycled sixty miles that day in vain.

About four years later I met Tricia by chance on a Sunday afternoon in Dublin. She was there training to be a nurse. It was lovely seeing her again. We laughed and talked for a while and then she said they had to be back at the hospital. As she and her friends walked away I thought of the lovely kiss at the fair and the laughter of her schoolfriends. It seemed so long ago.

But on that day of great disappointment in Corofin, I had had no time to feel sorry for myself. I had a full life already, and the hard work was not a problem for me. Sure the problem was there wasn't enough time in the day for fun and the work put together. But I was never ready to settle down and accept my life as a farmer. My aunts and uncles had all worked on the farm as youngsters and when I went to see them they were forever reminding me about all the hard work they'd put in. On and on they went about it. Even my uncle, who I was very fond of, Mick Daly was his name, would be giving out to me about how he never had anything out of all the work he did on the farm. I wasn't interested. I was too young and excited about life's adventures, and their complaints made up my mind for me that if they were this grumpy already, what would I be like when I was their age?

I was henceforth determined that my life would be different, with laughter, craic and fun.

So my next ambition was to be a pop star, an Irish Elvis. I'd have my hair combed back straight, and looking as much like him as I could. I did spend a fair amount of time contemplating travelling to America and taking the States by surprise with a mix of Irish music, singing and culture. These would be my quieter, winter thoughts: I'm going to head off and become quite famous out in America. But more even than music I wanted to be a film star. I had no idea how I'd go about it, but that was another strong ambition, to become an actor.

There was a cinema in Ennistymon, not a permanent cinema but a projector and screen set up in the town hall, little seats, only tuppence or threepence to go in. The owner was very irascible, and the projector was always breaking down. The minute the thing stopped working we'd start banging our feet on the timber floor. The owner would be furious. He'd rush into the main hall and of course the moment he opened the door everyone had stopped. When the projector got running again, I'd be engrossed by the cowboys films like *The High Chaparral*, and studying the actors.

Among my friends, I was the only one who had any such notion of becoming an actor. The others would normally be talking about girls or cows or cars, which I was happy to talk about as well, but nobody I knew saw themselves as an actor or even gave a damn about acting, so I could never discuss it with anyone. Then I had the chance to join the local dramatic group. Every year we'd do one or two three-act plays, starting in October by rehearsing one night a week, then December two nights a week and building up to a performance in March.

One year we staged a comedy called *Anyone Can Rob a Bank*. My part was as an English salesman staying as a guest in a B&B. The daughter of the house was a good-looking girl, and the English guest fancied her, as did the local Guard. Of course the Guard hated the Englishman, who was me, and was always telling her to have nothing to do with me, constantly blackening my name.

At one point in the play, the Guard had just left the house, and the daughter was sitting pensively on a little stool. I came downstairs, sat down by the side of her and put my arms around her. She was still thinking about what the Guard had been saying about me, which was nothing good. She mightn't have liked what he had said but she had listened to him and so was a little apprehensive and not as receptive to my attentions. As I sat there I looked out into the audience and saw that the first row of seats was full of priests, with two or three rows of nuns sitting just behind them.

The next thing, the door burst open and the girl's father came in. 'What are you doing there with my daughter?' 'Ah,' I said, 'I was just testing her love, just testing her love.'

And a voice came from the back of the theatre, 'Ah, you were just testing her tits!'

The whole audience roared. I remember looking down at the priests and they were enjoying it so much, but the nuns were pretending to be shocked of course, turning to each other and tutting, 'Oh that's awful.' I often think of the priests' expressions. Every single one of them was smiling.

When these plays came to an end each April, then I would get very busy again with farm work, the turf and the bog and the gardens, and I would think, Jesus, what am I going to do now that's all gone, missing all this excitement and fun?

Priest, soldier, musician, actor, I had all these plans for a change in my life, but sometimes the change that happens to you is something that no one could predict. I learnt this from a match I inadvertently made in my twenties. There was a wild lad I knew called Tommy, wild like Mickey who became a priest. Tommy had been thinking about going to England, but first he asked me did I know any women with land? I told him that I knew various farmers' daughters but only one woman with a good farm and some security, a widow called Peggy, though I told him to think hard about looking for a wife, saying, 'Tommy, you might have great fun in England.'

He was perhaps seven years older than me, in his late twenties, and had been adopted as a child so no one knew much of his background. In general what I knew I liked, especially his madness and wildness. I didn't know whether he should be staying in Ireland. He felt he needed more freedom. But he seemed now quite set on the idea of marrying the widow – and I was sure he was only interested in her money. And the more I realised that, the less my heart was in this match, because the woman was quite old, frail and in bad health, and a decent soul. Nevertheless I told a niece of hers to tell her about Tommy, and she quickly agreed to meet him as she needed someone to work the farm. She instantly liked him, and Tommy laughed at everything Peggy said.

A rusty old bike that had belonged to her husband was leaning up against a wall. Tommy went over, grabbed the bike and rode it around the rough yard, laughing like a clown. She showed us the cows, calves, geese and horses, and asked Tommy if he could drive as she was thinking of getting a tractor. At this Tommy looked extremely interested, as at the time almost no one owned their own tractor.

After not much ado the match was made. Tommy had been a farm labourer, badly paid and treated. Now he would have his own farm, bigger than the man's he had been working for. As we were leaving she said, 'Take the bike, Tommy.' He carried me back home on the crossbar. We rode over ditches and up on walls, and now I couldn't stop laughing either.

The day of their wedding quickly approached. It seemed as if Tommy laughed louder and stronger. I wondered what was in his head. On his wedding day he looked very dashing. Peggy had told him there was a good suit and shoes in the wardrobe – I suppose they were her late husband's. The church event was simple and it was different to see such a fine man with an older lady. Tommy and Peggy went off to the seaside for the day, and when they came back in the evening there was a big party at the farm.

The dancing started about nine o'clock. The floor was made of flags and in those times most men wore hobnail boots. The sound of the floor was magic. When a flag floor is laid, an old empty pot with the bottom gone is often placed underneath the flags to create a kind of echo chamber which will help the sound of the dancing ring out – you can do the same with a cow's skull buried beneath the floor. As the saying goes, empty vessels make more sound.

I danced a few sets and an old-time waltz with Peggy. Tommy was dancing with a dark-haired young girl, Aisling Davies. Peggy saw this and got a bad dose of the green-eyed monster, pulled Aisling away from Tommy and stormed off into a side room. One of her neighbours spotted this and followed Peggy into the room. 'Listen to me now,' she told Peggy. 'Give Tommy a taste of his own medicine. I'll tell you what to do. You know Joe Harrington, who was mad to court you years ago? Well, he's after buying a set of chickens in Spancil Hill last weekend. He's very proud of them, so what you do is go over and say, "How are you, Joe? I heard you bought a set of chickens the other week."'

'But how is that going to help?' asked Peggy.

'Just trust me. And keep this to yourself now, Peggy, keep this to yourself.'

Peggy did as she was told and went over to Joe, a sprightly old man, and asked him as instructed about his chickens. He was delighted at the opportunity to boast about his new pride and joy. 'Well, there's four hens,' he said, 'lovely white speckled things, and a beautiful cock. You'd want to see him, Peggy. You'll have to come up and watch him standing proud some day.' With that, Tommy, who was passing by where they were talking, caught the last part of the conversation, leapt to the wrong conclusion and started pulling Joe out for a fight.

Then Mary, the sister of Peggy's dead husband, leapt up and started shouting at her, 'You silly auld doting fool of a woman! Your deceased husband promised this farm and the land to my son in return for all the years he worked on the garden, in the meadows and out in the bog, and now you're acting like a silly teenager.' She slapped Peggy across the face. Peggy caught her by the hair on her head and together they crashed right across the dance floor.

A few people rushed to stop the cat fight but what surprised me most was that more people egged the two women on, with shouts of 'Let them at it!', 'Go on, Peggy!' 'Give it to her, Peggy!' The two women got up but fell into a dresser, bringing all the cups and candles and plates crashing down. Mary made a run for the door, Peggy ran after her and the fight was taken outside into the yard, with the crowd following to see the spectacle of these two women fighting like two ganders; they'd given up trying to separate them.

The excitement was such that no one noticed that back in the kitchen a lighted candle had been knocked on to some newspapers on the floor and now the curtains were ablaze.

Shouts went up: 'The house is on fire, the house is on fire!'
Everyone rushed back into the house, grabbing buckets and
saucepans to fill from barrels of water just outside the door
and desperately trying to put out the fire as it was a thatched
roof. All of a sudden the fight was forgotten about and everyone worked together to get the fire under control. The house
was saved, a huge sense of relief descended and for one
moment there was complete silence.

I suggested we all say a decade of the rosary to thank God
that the house wasn't completely destroyed. Mary, who minutes before had been fighting with Peggy, was always the
appointed person to start the rosary and prayers at funerals
and wakes. When I asked her to do this she was slow to
respond but, seeing everyone on their knees ready for prayer,
and perhaps afraid that some other ambitious woman would
steal this important role, she started the first mystery of the
rosary. Tommy placed a cushion on the floor for Peggy to
kneel on and was now kneeling beside her himself, all
thoughts and jealousies left outside. After the first 'Our
Father' and three Hail Marys were said a loud racket could
be heard outside in the yard. The strawboys, masked musicians and dancers, had arrived.

Mary did not attempt to hide her smile at the irony of
this, as the strawboys were a sign of fertility in this particular
locality. I thought Tommy would have his work cut out for
him in that department, as Peggy was far beyond her child-
bearing years. The strawboys squared up for the first dance,

which started with whoops, whistles and shouts of relief: a Caledonian set of four reels, a jig and a hornpipe. By the end of six different sets nobody had any energy left. The strawboys banged on the floor and shouted loudly, 'Good luck to the bride, good luck to the bride!' A few seconds of silence were broken by an old woman shouting from the parlour door, 'C'mon for tea and sandwiches.' Refreshed, the dancers started off again, and more sets of strawboys arrived during the course of the night. The music was still playing when I left at eight-thirty in the morning.

In the remaining years I only saw Tommy a couple of times. I had heard that he had gotten the tractor, and had marvellous pleasure out of the farm. Peggy meanwhile was radiantly happy with her young husband. But one day, when Tommy was changing the wheel on the tractor it had toppled over on top of him, crushing his leg and leaving him unable to walk without help.

The last time I saw Tommy and Peggy they were arriving at Mass with a fine horse and cart. Even though Peggy was getting on by this time, she was the one who jumped down and went around the other side to assist Tommy down. I couldn't believe how old, frail and pale Tommy looked as Peggy handed him two walking sticks. He was as bent as those bushes out along the road to Ennistymon, their backs turned for shelter against the winds from the west. The change was remarkable: the couple seemed to have swapped places, she getting younger as he grew old. As Tommy hobbled into the church, Peggy was positively bounding along beside him.

Faith obviously has its own agenda, I thought, and my fortune-telling activities crossed my mind. Whenever I was reading palms I was right more times than not, by skill or sheer luck, and I found that people at the festival, especially those who knew about my father and grandfather being matchmakers, would go out of their way to track me down and ask me when they would find love. It did occur to me that, after all my other dreams, maybe my own fortune was coming to find me.

4
Something in the Lisdoonvarna Air

As I approached my twenties, I was spending much of my time at the Lisdoonvarna festival every autumn, shadowed by the ghost of my grandfather and the reputation of my father, and constantly asked to help engineer romantic liaisons. But I still had no intention of taking up the mantle of the Daly matchmaking tradition. I was young, I was free, and I wanted to spend my time gallivanting about like any other young blood would. I was having the time of my life.

I even had my first car. I was nineteen when I bought this old van for the princely sum of £100. It was magic, and opened up a whole new world. With my friends I travelled over to Ennis, to Limerick, to Kilkee and even to Galway to go to dances. Although the van was new to me, it was really quite antiquated, and didn't have any locks on the doors. So my van was often commandeered by young couples on wet nights for kisses, cuddles and courting, and it became known as the Passion Wagon.

My friend and I met two girls in Ennis and we dated a few times. There was always a third girl called Theresa with them, and we told her we would find a nice boy for her. One night we brought another friend, Denny, a farm worker, along with us. On the way to Ennis in the van to pick up the girls we told Denny we'd fix him up with this girl Theresa. He replied that he had never had a girl and wouldn't know what to do. My other friend said, in devilment, 'Ach, didn't you often seen the bull bullin' a cow?', which was our delicate local term for bulls doing what bulls like to do when they start feeling frisky.

Theresa was the daughter of a farmer, but was now a college student and told me she didn't want to be with a farmer's son. Jokingly I said to her, 'Denny's studying to be a doctor, but he's awful shy.' Once in a while, you may notice, I might bend the truth a little, but all in the name of romance, of course.

Well, we danced the night away and when the time came to go home Denny got into the Passion Wagon beside Theresa. He said not a word. Eventually my other friend placed Denny's arm around Theresa's shoulders to encourage him, and with this Denny got overexcited and grabbed Theresa, throwing his arms around her. She was startled and drew back a little, saying, 'Excuse me, Denny, but I would really like to be wooed.'

At this, Denny, mishearing what she said and remembering our advice about the bull and the cow, immediately started bellowing, 'Moo, moo, moo,' and scraping his foot like a hoof across the floor of the van. Then Theresa opened the door, jumped out and fled; we never saw her, or indeed the other two girls, again. There obviously was still some way for me to go in refining my matchmaking skills.

Still, from time to time some of the older folk would come up to me and say, 'Willie, why don't you do the matchmaking now?', but I'd always make a noncommittal answer, avoid the question, say something like 'Oh, I haven't really given it any thought.'

A small drop of matchmaker's advice

♡ *I recently had a young man of twenty approach me during the Matchmaking Festival and ask me to help him make a match. He was extremely shy on his own and wanted to find somebody his age that he could feel comfortable talking to. It made me think back to my days as a young man. And I realised that although I was actually quite shy, having people around who helped make me confident was the key. I suggested that this young man return the following day with a friend or two. The next evening he turned up with his brother and two friends. As soon as he showed up he already seemed different.*

There was a group of girls in from Dublin and I suggested that the two groups come into my 'office' at the Matchmaker Bar for a pint. Well, it worked like a charm. Within fifteen minutes the boys were asking the girls to dance and the shy young man was on the dance floor, talking more than dancing. Every now and then I'd see his brother or one of his friends check to see how he was doing and I could see that having them close by had given him a sense of security in this new adventure. ♡

Although I was enjoying myself as a young chancer in Lisdoonvarna, I had no idea that the Matchmaking Festival would become such an important part of my life.

If you are single and open to finding a match, you really shouldn't let another year pass by without going to Lisdoonvarna. Even if you're not on the look-out for a little romance, it's an extraordinary event to be part of, and the craic is simply marvellous.

Each September, as the shadows lengthen and the harvesting days have finished, thousands of single men and women come to the Matchmaking Festival. There is noise and excitement in the dances and the pubs and out on the streets, as everyone goes out looking for fun and for love.

Lisdoonvarna has all the ingredients for matchmaking. People in the mood for romance, knowing that most everybody else there has come for the same reason. Plenty of places to meet, the hotel lobbies, the dance halls, the bars. And large amounts of drink to encourage the meek and befuddle the brave.

For eleven months of the year you could drive straight though the quiet centre of Lisdoonvarna and never once suspect that come September the place will be heaving with gaiety. It is, and always has been, a small market town.

On market days people from round about would come into the town to sell produce, buy goods for themselves and then head back out, nothing more or less than that. There were certainly no tourists.

Although the quality of the waters from the springs at Lisdoonvarna were well known, it was not until sometime during the 1870s that doctors and scientists analysed their mineral content. They discovered that the waters contained high levels of iodine, hydrogen sulphide, lithium, iron, calcium and manganese, all of which were very beneficial to health, for everything from rheumatism and gout to bronchitis and liver complaints. A spa and baths were built and around them a number of small guest-houses and hotels started setting up.

You can still buy a pint of the waters to drink in the pump house. The old spa health centre offered various treatments, including a bath in the sulphur waters where a small electric charge was applied to your toes every few minutes from a car battery. More like a torture than a rest cure! Personally I never took the waters of Lisdoonvarna that often. The sulphur smell never appealed to me, although I would on occasion force a quarter of a glass or so down, hoping the promise of health would come true.

As Lisdoonvarna's renown grew, farmers from Tipperary, Cork or Westmeath heard about the medicinal benefits of taking the waters and, since County Clare was also known for good music, they began to come and stay during the autumn once the harvest was over. They came from counties with good green pasture (Clare was considered poor enough land, which is why we would produce stock to sell on to farmers with better-quality land) and could afford to take a short break to recover from months of hard work and whiskey drinking.

A farmer from Tip might be staying in a hotel or guest-house and mention over breakfast, 'My son Johnny is twenty-eight and I must get him on,' or 'I've Peggy, now, she's twenty-four and still not married,' or there'd be an aunt looking for a wife for a shy nephew. That was how it went. And it just so happened that, not so very far away in Ballingaddy, there was a matchmaker called William Daly.

Gradually the matchmaking activity became as much of a draw as the fabled waters. It was said that because the town is high on a hill, there were breezes from all four points of the compass – so it was hardly surprising that love was in the air. Each year the celebrations grew and grew and outstripped and outlasted all the other towns that had similar events. By the end of the 1890s, new railway lines and steamers from Galway were bringing tens of thousands of visitors every September, and the place became known as 'the Cheltenham of Ireland'.

Once the locals realised what was up, the word would go round among the men from Clare who were thinking it was time they got married. A friend or a cousin would say, 'Why don't you go down to Quinlan's or Garvin's? That's where the matchmaker is.' And off they'd go.

By the time I was born, the impromptu matchmaking at the spa had turned into a month-long festival, and of course this brought more business to my father's door. Year-round, people would be stopping by, but there were always plenty more when the Lisdoonvarna festivities began. The first week would be quite slow in starting, but by the second and third weeks the activity was intense, before waning over the final fortnight.

There were so many great characters at Lisdoonvarna, like the couple of fellas from Tipperary who would come down for one particular week during the festival. The one who we called the Templemore Greyhound was well over eighty, but still dancing like hell. And the other, known as the Neenagh Splinter, spent all the time boasting about all the women he was out with.

There was one woman called Annie I used to see at Lisdoonvarna. Annie was intent, consistent and didn't understand the word 'no'. She was tall, with big square shoulders, and wore a long salt-and-pepper overcoat with the belt tied about her waist. She usually carried a big oblong leather bag similar to the ones tradesmen used to carry tools to work in. She was always with two older ladies who were quite ladylike and refined.

I usually came across Annie after the morning dance at the wells. She would seem to come out of nowhere, grab my wrist and ask me to read her palm. She had a grip like a vice. There was no getting away, and always the same question: 'Can you see a man in my palm?'

'Maybe, Annie, maybe.'

The next question would be 'What does he look like?'

Over the years I had described an array of different men I would see in her palm. Her two friends would say, 'Willie, she likes you.' I would laugh and say nothing. I would still have the mark of her hand on my wrist for some time.

One morning I ran into Annie outside the dance, and she seized my wrist yet again. She didn't beat about the bush, and said directly, 'Willie, I met no man.' I was with two men in there, late forties one, the other late fifties. She looked at them and said, 'I don't want a farmer.' Looking back I should have said, 'But you'd make a great farmer's wife. You're so strong.' But, being in the mood for fun, I introduced Tommy as a doctor and Pad Joe as a pilot. With that she dropped the bag she was carrying with such ease on my foot, almost breaking my big toe, grabbed Pad Joe and pulled him out for a slow waltz. She swung and turned him, she held him close.

He was tiny compared to Annie so she hugged him into her, and as she whirled him around all you could see was his smile and a little glint in one eye. All his friends were laughing like hell of course.

I said to myself, I'd better not tell her Pad Joe's a farmer or she'll throw him out of the window. A number of people almost tripped over her bag on the ground. With the assistance of another man we moved it to one side. As the zip was not completely closed, I could see about a dozen pint bottles in it. Initially I thought it must be stones. I enquired of her two friends what was in the bottles. They whispered, 'She has "sulphur water" written on them, but they are bottles of holy water.'

It was two years till I met Annie again. As usual she took me by surprise, and again coming up from the sulphur wells. I was ushered to an empty seat, her two friends always within hearing distance of the palm-reading. They were sweet really, analysing and openly approving of what was said. Sometimes Annie would look at them but not speak. With her big hand outstretched she quickly said, 'Can you see a man there?'

I looked straight into her eyes and said, 'I do.' With that she took her other hand off my wrist as I started on her second question, 'What does he look like?'

Her friends had told me she worked for the civil service in Dublin. I said she was going to marry a tall dark handsome young man.

She said, 'I have never met anyone like that. Will I meet him in Lisdoonvarna?'

'No, he works in the office,' I said.

'There's no one in the office like that.'

Like that, one of her friends interrupted: 'Annie, what about that new lad from Sligo who's started taking round the teas?'

'But he never looks at me,' Annie said.

I took my chance: 'He's mad in love with you but too shy to say.'

'How do you know?' she replied.

I said, 'It's here in your palm.' Her two friends moved close.

'What else can you see? How many children will I have?'

I looked closely at her palm and said, 'Seven. You'll have four with your husband and you're going to have an affair with another man and have three with him,' messing with her.

She said very seriously, 'I'd never do that,' but in the same breath asked, 'What does this other man look like?'

I said, 'A small, fat, bald man.'

She quickly replied, 'I hate men like that.'

Then one of her friends asked, 'What does he work at?'

I said, 'He's a professional gambler. You'll be going to all the race meetings and become addicted to gambling.'

Annie said, 'I've never gambled in my life,' then, 'How soon will I marry?'

'In six months,' I replied. Annie got up, called her friends, and said, 'Let's go.'

Time passed, and another couple of years later I was coming up the steps at the wells again. I could hear someone shouting, 'Willie! Willie!' Looking back I saw Annie's two friends. I quickly looked left and right but Annie was not to be seen.

They said, 'Willie, lovely to see you, how are you?'

'Great, great. Is Annie with ye?' I asked a little nervously.

They said, 'Do you not know? Annie and the boy from the office got married shortly after you spoke to her.'

I was delighted. Apparently she had gone back to Dublin and they had become close; the lad was from the country and was probably lonely in the city, which can be very cold, and I suppose she had more than a little warmth in her. I often think about Annie and am glad that she found the right man for her.

A small drop of matchmaker's advice

♡ *Annie's story showed me that part of the job of a matchmaker is to encourage people to open their eyes and look in what might seem a less obvious direction – and that includes me. I had started off assuming, because of her physical build, that Annie would be looking for a hefty farmer, but once she told me that she had other expectations I had to help her look around her. We had had a little fun pretending the little old farmer was a pilot, but in the end, by suggesting she consider someone she had not thought about in a romantic way – or had not admitted to herself she had feelings for – she found the love that had been eluding her. We tend to get trapped so easily into a predictable way of thinking. If you can manage to break that pattern, more than likely you'll be pleasantly surprised. ♡*

When I was very young and going to Lisdoonvarna it was not yet formally known as the Matchmaking Festival. There were very few people of my own age, say fifteen or sixteen, there. There is still an older crowd at the festival, who attend the afternoon dances at the spa wells. Some of them are already married but turn up at the festival with a single person's spirit, the women booking into the B&Bs with friends as if they're on a hen night. Their husbands will also be in Lisdoonvarna but staying at a different B&B with their friends. They don't make any plans to meet their other half, although they may well bump into each other along the way. It's a strange phenomenon.

Although I was much younger than most of the festival-goers, I always found something intriguing to draw me back. I was tall and women admired me. And there was dancing at four or five different venues, in a few of the hotels and a couple of dance halls.

I once went with a friend who was a Guard. There was a huge demand to get into all the dances, but he told me, 'Don't worry, Willie, I've got my official badge.' We went to the first venue, and there was no way in. The second venue was the same, so when we went down to the Kincora Dance Hall, he flashed his badge. It made absolutely no difference!

The proprietress at the Hydro Hotel liked me and my friends for some reason. There would be a massive queue outside, a hundred people waiting to get in, but if ever she saw us she'd wave us over: 'Come on, lads, come in.' We were young, we liked dancing, and we would start to stir up some excitement, so it suited her to let us in for free to get some atmosphere created.

At the Kincora Dance Hall there was a little pocket window just inside the front door where you had to pay. Since we never had any money, we used to wait for a big old man with a large coat to go in. We'd slip him a little bit of cash to stand in front of the window and pretend to be searching for some change. Meanwhile we'd slip in behind him – for the price of his entry we might get half a dozen of us to slide in unnoticed.

Lisdoonvarna was a mad party. Most of the people were from other counties, not on our own doorstep, so you were free to let your hair down. That said, the incomers were there for a few days over one weekend; I was there for the whole thirty-five days. So I would pace myself. But I enjoyed it immensely and I always made sure I got involved. Many of the other locals would go to the Irish Arms and the Roadside Tavern – the two pubs they always went to, month in, month out – and let the festival swirl on around their heads.

They were missing out on some great fun, and some great music, because Lisdoonvarna always attracted wonderful musicians. At the dance halls and the Pavilion some of the most famous show-bands came through, and they often had a guest artist, like Maggie Barry, a brilliant ballad street singer, who had a marvellous style of singing, crystal clear. One singer in the Royal Spa Hotel intrigued me, a very fine entertainer called Pecker Don, who played banjo and fiddle. Pecker's songs were a little unusual, all about tinkers and travellers, like 'Sullivan's John to the Road You're Gone' – 'you're gone to the tinker's daughter and along the road to Rome'. Another of the Lisdoonvarna musicians I got to know well was Ted Furey, a great character and fiddle player. His sons were also musicians and achieved fame as the Furey Brothers. Ted was very proud of them. The first time I saw the boys with him, the great surprise was I didn't even know he was married! And I thought, 'Jesus, when does he ever see the kids, he's in Lisdoonvarna all the time.'

Another regular was Patsy Whelan, on guitar and fiddle, who was a couple of years younger than me. We all became very close friends, and sometimes I would sing in their company, perhaps 'The Spanish Lady', a lovely tune: 'As I walked down through Dublin City at the hour of twelve at night, who would I see but the Spanish Lady washing her feet by candle light. When she saw me she did flee me, lifting her petticoat over her white knee. In all my life I never did see a girl so pretty as the Spanish Lady . . .'

Music has always been part of my life. I still have my parents' old gramophone in the sitting room. That was what we listened to music on mainly, using 78s. Both my sisters played the piano and took lessons, while I played the tin whistle at school from about nine or ten. Our teacher at the time was young, and instead of concentrating on the Catechism he was spending lessons showing us how to play the whistle.

Then it came time for Confirmation. It was the most embarrassing day of the teacher's life, I'd say. The bishop and the canon were visiting two schools: Kilshanny, where all the students knew everything, and ours, where we knew nothing. The bishop and canon tossed a coin to see who'd go to which school, and we got the bishop, which was even worse. We'd never seen anyone looking like that in our entire lives, a huge man looming over us in funny clothes, a great pink outfit of robes and ropes, and a massive pink hat way up on his head. All of us young lads were terrified.

Up he went to this first boy, one of a dozen or more brothers, and asked him a question, but he was so shy he couldn't answer. The bishop moved on to his younger brother and he wouldn't answer either, so the teacher was going up and down making excuses: 'They're a big family,' and this and that. But it snowballed. Everyone panicked. The priest came down after that and all the tin whistles were taken away. And we were examined for the Catechism unfailingly every day for the next two years. Luckily they couldn't confiscate my love for music as easily. I still play some guitar, the *bodhrán* (the traditional single-sided goatskin drum) and the whistle too. I owned a pub called Daly's in Ennistymon for many years, with regular live music, and was always happy to get up and play there.

Now to prove that the magic of romance remains as strong as it ever was in these parts, and that the power of music is as seductive and as beneficial as the waters of Lisdoonvarna, let me tell you the story of Michael and Phyllis.

A couple of years back Michael, a man I already knew as a great fiddle player, approached me. He was in his late thirties, a fine tall guy, but he'd let himself go a bit. His mother, who he'd been living with, had died a year or so before, and she'd been the one who kept him in good nick, ironing his shirts and looking after him generally. Now he'd grown a bit rakish, a little careless in his appearance, and between you and me was quite fond of the drink. However, Michael realised he was in danger of getting out of control, so he came up to me one evening after we'd both been playing in one of the pubs in Doolin and said, 'Willie, you have to find me a wife.'

'I'll try my best, Michael, I always do.'

Shortly afterwards a group of American women came out for a week's pony-trekking. The girls leading the trek always pointed me out – 'That's Willie, the matchmaker' – and this obviously intrigued one of the women, a thirty-year-old from Boston called Phyllis, because she popped by to introduce herself to me. 'The rest of the group are all married,' she said, 'but I'm not spoken for. Do you know any men who might be suitable?'

I mentioned the conversation to Michael later that week, and he invited me to take Phyllis up to meet him.

I picked Phyllis up from her B&B and we headed out way up into the hills where Michael lived. It was a gorgeous June evening. Out here in the far west it's light until very late. The roadway up to the house looked neglected, a track originally built for a donkey and cart, narrow, winding, the walls close in, but the trees overhanging it were enchanting.

'Oh, Willie, I could never live here,' Phyllis told me at least three times as we bumped along the lane. 'It's far too quiet. I'm a city girl.' But as we got to within a few minutes of Michael's place, the summer breeze carried us the strains of a fiddle playing, and we stopped to listen to the music among the briars and bushes. I recognised a couple of the tunes he was playing, a lovely jig, 'The Lark in the Morn', and a beautiful air called 'The Lonesome Boatman'. I could see the music was working some kind of magic on Phyllis.

We arrived in front of the house. Michael was sitting on a large stone outside his door. When he saw Phyllis a big smile came to his face, and he started playing a reel. Then he stopped, turned to me and said, 'Jesus, Willie, you've brought me a lovely woman,' put his hands out and whisked Phyllis off in a little dance.

Inside the house, which was full of lovely old furniture, a dresser with cups, a fresh tablecloth on the table, he set his violin and bow down and poured us some tea. Phyllis still hadn't said a word. But once she and Michael started talking they barely stopped. Two nights later I saw them together in our pub, Michael looking very spruce. And the power of the music continued to work its charm, because they're now married and living in Boston, where of an evening you can still from time to time hear Michael in one of the Irish pubs, playing 'The Lonesome Boatman' on his fiddle, the tune that helped bring them together – with a little help from their good friend Willie Daly the matchmaker, of course.

I can remember the moment when, after all these years of reading palms, making a few matches, playing music and having fun, it struck me that there was a genuine need for somebody to carry on the matchmaking work of the Daly family. I can't pinpoint precisely the day – it was early one morning in 1966 or thereabouts – but I do know exactly where it was. I had walked up on to the hills behind the house and was standing there looking across the fields all around.

It was the day after an auction where the household effects of a man I knew well, Tommy, a lovely larger-than-life character and a great wit, had been sold after his death. On a few occasions Tommy had said to me, 'Willie Daly, will you get me a wife?' But though Tommy was a fine-looking man, dark ringlets hanging down over his face and a look in his younger years like Jack Palance, he was, I thought, fonder of the drink than of the women. Sometimes I'd hear him cursing about women as he rolled out of the pub. 'Let 'em go to hell, let 'em go to hell.' So I took no notice. But then he'd be back asking me to get him a wife.

As I stood on the hillside it dawned on me that maybe Tommy had actually meant it, and that I had not acted on his wishes. As I looked around I could see other houses where there were bachelors, like Tommy the end of their line, whose name would disappear along with them if they did not get married and have children.

I also had a strong sense of tradition, even if I was more modern-minded than my parents' generation. I was the last to get a tractor in the area, enjoying the work with the horses. I always liked the old-style thatched cottages, and was disappointed when the government offered substantial grants to change the thatch to slates – most people were quick enough to take the money. Even when I was a boy of ten or eleven I felt the same. I sat one evening listening to a friend of my father's tell him, 'God of glory tonight, Henry, 'tis a bad man who wouldn't take the thatch off his house and build a hay shed for his son.' What a shame, I thought.

My father had been carrying on with the matchmaking even into his seventies, and that was part of the reason I had felt no real pressure to inherit that part of our family life. But by the time I was in my twenties he had started going quite deaf, growing stooped as well, and felt awkward being out in public. It was clear that at some point he would have to give up the matchmaking completely.

With all the changes under way in the 1960s more and more of the young folk were moving away to the cities. We would be losing lovely friends, neighbours and families. I did even worry about our own farm. I was aware that I was the only male Daly left from a very big number of families. And that's when I made up my mind that I should take the matchmaking more seriously and give it a real go. I haven't stopped since.

5
The Swing of Things

Having made my decision to continue the Daly tradition, I knew I had to adapt my style of matchmaking to the changing times. We had left the 1950s and were well into the Swinging Sixties, and even though our main street in Ennistymon might have been maybe a couple of decades behind Carnaby Street, the shift in attitudes was not so slow to reach us. The Beatles even came to Ennistymon. It's true!

I was twenty when the Beatles first arrived in Ireland in the November of 1963. I was over in Dublin visiting some of our relatives and walking by myself down O'Connell Street, towards where the Adelphi cinema stood. The whole street was packed with young people, there was a terrible roaring. 'What's all the crowd for?' I asked another fella.

'Don't you know? The Beatles are down at the Adelphi.'

That didn't stir my emotions too much, to be honest,

though of course I knew about Beatlemania from the papers. I went further down the street, and stumbled into what was rapidly turning into a mini-riot. Youngsters were picking cars up – Morris Minors and VWs – by the back wheels and turning them upside-down. The Guards arrived in a black van and started shoving the crowd back and forth, linking arms to make a cordon and telling the youngsters to back off. There was a girl of seventeen or so who flipped the cap off a Guard in his mid-thirties and brushed his nose. He belted her. I saw one bunch of lads setting fire to a double-decker bus.

The following Easter I was back home and trying to get an old car fixed. The gearbox had gone, so I headed into town as there was a fella there who had a replacement ready for me. I drove in with the taxi driver Paddy Marrion, but when I was ready to go back Paddy said, 'Look, I'm going to pick up some women to take them out to Moher, it will take me about half an hour. Can you wait for me to get back?' 'Fair enough.' An hour passed. I was waiting outside G. Connolly, sitting on a wall. Across the street I noticed a couple of guys in white Aran sweaters walking with Monica Woods, who was the daughter of the proprietor of the Falls Hotel. She was older, a lovely girl.

After a while the word went out that these guys in white sweaters were two of the Beatles. They popped into Considine's the saddlers and Conway's shop, and wandered about looking at the knick-knacks on sale there. A young cousin of mine came up to me, excited that the Beatles were in town. 'Go on, go and get an autograph,' I said. There were only two more people in that whole hour I was waiting who went near them, even though it was a busy Saturday, with lots of people out shopping. I couldn't tell if the Beatles were happy that they were not being bothered, or disappointed that they weren't. They weren't used to the lack of attention. It turned out that they had been staying in Dromoland Castle down near Newmarket-in-Fergus near Shannon, and later had to be smuggled out in baskets to a laundry van to avoid the crowds who came up from Ennis and Limerick once the news got out that the Beatles were there. They'd headed up to our corner of Clare to get a little peace and quiet.

Paddy Marrion turned up in his taxi with the women. 'Willie, hop in.' We arrived in Liscannor. 'I'm heading for Moher now,' Paddy said. 'Shall I leave you here and pick you up later, while I'm dropping the women off?' I went into McHugh's pub, which was also the general stores in the village, just opposite the harbour, and there was Monica Woods again, with her sister Kate, three or four other girls and the Beatles; they were busy taking photos of Joe's store walls. The tiny shop sold everything: there was brandy and rat poison next to the bread, bacon, forks and rakes, shovels, oats, bowls and nails. Monica came over to me, as we were good friends of the Woods family, and introduced me to her new-found acquaintances: 'Willie, this is John and George.' They gathered round me and we talked for a minute, quite friendly. The lads were asking me about the local quarries – after all, they had once been the Quarrymen! – and the stone walls in

Liscannor, because between each house there was a high stone wall, which was odd in a small village.

Back inside the bar, a man was trying to sing a song called 'Dear Old Skibbereen' that I sometimes sing too: 'They say it is a lovely land, wherein a prince might dwell. So why did you abandon it, the reason to me tell . . .' But this fella was drunk and couldn't manage to make it past the first verse. Joe McHugh, the proprietor, shouted up to me, 'Willie, why don't you get up and sing?' I walked down to the bar, leaving the Beatles in the front of the shop. Joe hadn't even noticed them. He asked me again, 'Willie, why don't you sing?'

I said, 'Well, them lads above might sing for you.'

He took one look at them and said dismissively, 'Ah, they're only tourists, they wouldn't have a note in their heads!' Joe never knew how close he was to having his own private concert by the Beatles.

I had already had my own taste of how quickly things were changing when I took my first trip to England, when I went there to work on the building sites in the winter of 1960–61, an experience that opened my eyes to the world beyond our farm. I think it was the first time I ever heard the word 'sex' spoken out loud. We really were all pretty innocent back then, and there was just no mention of the word. It was a cardinal sin if you did. There was a lot of mystery about it all. A parent would never dare bring up the subject, and it dawns on me now that one of the few times that there would be a tiny bit more liberal talk and banter than on any other occasion was at the plucking of the gander, as the older women fussed over the bride-to-be. You'd see one of the women pinching the young girl's breast, tweaking her arse a little bit, that would be very common, and they'd be laughing and laughing as they hinted at what lay in store after she got married.

There was an old belief, a superstition, that a man should not sleep with his wife for the first week after their wedding, or they would never be blessed with children. The groom, it was said, should go to bed with his trousers on back to front, just to make sure. They said it helped ease the fears of young girls who might be scared by the prospect of sleeping with her new husband, particularly if he was a bit older then her, as was common. After five nights lying with him in the bed, she might decide it wasn't so terrible after all.

To give you an idea of how naive we were, that first time I went over to England, when I was almost eighteen, I needed some new trousers, so I popped into a department store. A salesgirl came up to me and asked if she could help me. I said I wanted to buy some trousers and was interested in this particular pair. 'Oh, that's a nice pair of trousers,' she said, 'they're unisex.' As soon as she said the word 'unisex' I put the pants straight back down, left them there and walked out of the store in a state of shock, thinking, Jesus, all I wanted to do was buy some trousers and she starts talking about sex.

*

I was not a total innocent, of course. From a small child I was well aware of the possibilities of romance, from hearing stories and keeping my eyes open. One bright May morning, following an all-night party at one of the neighbouring houses, my mother and I were heading down to cross the river and we came across a couple sitting under a bush kissing and cuddling. I must have been nine, no older, and took my cue from my mother, who was far from shocked, but laughed as we walked past.

The first girls I was aware of were the ones who lived in Ballingaddy. On long summer evenings when I was six or seven I could hear laughter and shouting near our house as all the young kids gathered on a nearby hillside, known as Clare's Hill, to play hurling, using makeshift boards and sticks as a proper hurley was expensive. I was too young to participate so I would sit on the wall and watch. The family next to the field were the Crehans, Sean, Michael and Paddy, all fine hurlers. The Kearneys, who also lived right by the hill – Bridie, Nancy, Riona, PJ, Vincent and John – enjoyed the game as much. Eileen and Pat McInerney could see from their house when the game was on and would walk or cycle over. Then the Looney family would arrive, along with the Kelleghers, the Clancys and the O'Leary boys and girls. Sometimes the girls would take on the boys and often outdid them; Maura, the daughter of Mick Clare who owned the field, was a brilliant hurler. The girls were quite tough, but I always felt they were very good-looking, sweet and fun.

Many years after the laughter of the hurling stopped, we were all very proud when one of the local girls, little Marie McMahon, went to the Olympics and ran for Ireland.

My first more deliberate contact with local girls was at the crossroads at the end of our road. Kellys Cross it was called, because there were four Kellys living in each of the houses nearby. And all of them were called John Kelly, so to differentiate them one was known as Johnno, another Johnny John, and the others Sean Rua and Sean Dubh. Girls would come up from Ennistymon, which was three or four miles away, and we'd get friendly, though to be honest, at twelve and thirteen the girls were more interested in us than we were in them.

At the crossroads, if you liked a girl you'd sit her on the bar of your bicycle and talk of this and that, simple stuff, hours talking. But most of the time the girls would have to watch us being boys, kicking an old football, throwing stones from the road to try and smash the glass cups on the telegraph poles, practising hurling or playing pitch-and-toss. We'd chat to people passing up and down, with the odd horse or jaunting car. About five o'clock my father would be trying to get the cows back in, and as he was getting older and liked to have another pair of hands to help him with the job, he'd whistle for me. I'd hear the whistle and dash back home to give him a hand, leaving the girls behind.

If we had a free Sunday we would go over to Lahinch, the seaside resort, where we met a lot of girls coming up on the narrow-gauge train from Limerick, on what was called the 'Sea-breeze Special'. We spent three or four years as an unofficial reception committee for them. Before that we had been happy knowing the local girls. Suddenly there were these droves of lovely new girls coming up from Limerick and Ennis, and we'd be waiting diligently for them at the railway station.

The city girls we met at Lahinch were a little bit more modern in their dress and their attitudes than the girls from round about us. I remember the first time I saw one of the Limerick girls chewing gum, something I'd never seen before, and later they were the first girls to wear mini-skirts: the local girls were slow enough putting them on. What was unfair was that we'd spend all the time with the local girls during the winter up till the month of June, and it was lovely to have them to talk to. Then all these city girls would move in for the summer, and of course the novelty of the city girls was very exciting for me. When the summer finished and we went back to the local girls, they were quite rightly resentful, looking down their noses at us for running off to the city girls – 'Ah, you can feck off!'

We were very fortunate to have Lahinch so close to us. It was a great meeting spot, with typical seaside attractions and an amusement centre with swingboats, bumpers, and shooting ranges with little guns. Next to Lahinch golf course there was one part of the sandhills with long grass, quite sheltered. The run of it was that if you met a girl who liked you, you'd go off to the promenade for ice cream and then on to these sandhills. So on a Sunday, if we were lucky, we'd be scurrying off down the sandhills and then rushing back madly for the train before it left for Ennis and Limerick again.

When we were with a girl we would be trying to dodge her parents, who had spent the afternoon drinking. If we did bump into them, the mother would say angrily to their daughter, 'Where have you been, what are you at?' and the dads would say, 'Oh, leave April alone, leave the girl alone. She's all right.'

But mostly the parents were still in the pub. As well as girls chewing gum, those Sundays in Lahinch were the first time I had seen women in pubs. I once saw a husband and wife fighting: it took me a while to realise she was drunk. A later time, I came across another couple fighting. The man was hitting his wife in the face. He came at her again so I pushed him to the ground. She said to him, 'Are you hurt?' And then she swung around at me with her handbag: 'Don't ever fecking go near that man again!'

The train was scheduled to depart at 5.30 p.m., but everybody had to be on board before it could leave. Usually the children were all back on the train, but their parents weren't! It was hard work for the train crew. The driver and the ticket conductor would be pulling the adults out of the pubs. The adults wouldn't want to leave, they were having a good singsong. Eventually some of the parents would arrive, arm in arm, still singing. They'd get half of them up to the station and the other half would have set off back down into

Lahinch for another drink. So if you were late getting back from the sandhills, you knew the train would be at least a quarter of an hour late, maybe even an hour.

And on a Garland Sunday, the holiday that marked the end of summer, it was even worse: the pubs were completely packed and the train might not get away till half-nine or ten. The train crew would be shouting, 'This is your last chance,' there'd be a lot of effing and blinding, and then once the parents made it on to the train they'd pass out, and all you could hear was the sound of them snoring as the train rocked them fast asleep. Now everyone was happy, the driver and conductor, and the women happy their men were sleeping. The driver would start singing to the conductor and fireman, 'Are ye right there, Michael, are ye right? Do you think that we'll be there before the night?' And those still awake would sing back, 'Still ye might now, Michael, still ye might!'

I was fortunate with the girls. From a very early age I used to get on very well with them. I was going to the horse and cattle fairs to help my father, and at every fair there'd be rakes of girls coming up and chatting and talking to me. When I was fifteen, on Valentine's Day I walked out from a dedicated hard day's work and into a happy dreamworld. There were eleven Valentine's cards waiting for me. You can't imagine my surprise. I didn't know anything about them, didn't really know what a Valentine's card was in truth. Our postman, Leo Armistead, who was a great character, said,

'Jesus, Willie, the girls like you plenty,' and my mother could only laugh with shock and amazement. I was shocked and amazed too, and thrilled of course. I couldn't quite understand this, because I was so shy. Well, shy, sure, but willing.

When some of the more progressive sides of life in the sixties did find their way to Ireland, we were not always ready for them. One time I was up in Galway on holiday with my aunt and uncles. Their lifestyle was even more rural than ours in Clare. On this day we were making a big cock of hay. They used a pole in the centre to keep the hay standing, something we never did. The reason was that they were in sheep country, so as the sheep would eat at the base of the haycock the hay would fall evenly, guided by the pole.

Various neighbours had gathered to help. There would be great fun and craic. A man my uncle knew came by on an ass and cart selling poteen – which Galway was famous for – and had five bottles with him. My uncle said, 'Where's your brother Johnny? He should be here to make the *súgáns* to muggle the reek' – the small ropes of straw to hold the haycock together. Johnny turned up later, and when he saw him my uncle remarked, 'Begor, I've never seen Johnny in such good form.'

Johnny talked excitedly, and told me his story. He said, 'Willie, I thought I would need you to find me a woman, but things are looking up.'

'Good, good,' I said, 'always nice to see a man doing his own business.'

Johnny said, 'I was drawing hay for the Lawlers. And as I was passing the Paradise place, a young woman came out and asked me to come in.' Now the Paradise was a kind of retreat in the mountains where young people came from the city to unwind like hippies.

I asked Johnny, 'Was she good-looking?'

He said, 'She's gorgeous.'

Messing, I asked, 'So why didn't you go in?'

'I couldn't,' he said, 'I was working. I had the horse and float and hay with me.'

As he finished the thatching and muggling of the reek, Johnny seemed to be doing it all much faster than usual, and he was also drinking great gulps of poteen. He came over to me and said, 'Willie, what would you have done if she'd invited you in?' Putting his hand into his pocket, he pulled out a French letter and said, 'She gave me this too . . .' Half joking, half serious.

I said, 'Ah, Johnny, I'd reckon I'd definitely have gone in.'

He hesitated for a moment, then he said, 'You're right. I'll go home, have a wash, put it on me and get myself over to her.' I said nothing.

About one hour later I saw him as he flew past my uncle's house on his bike on his way to Paradise. I wondered if he did have the French letter in place, all set up. Ah, the joys of free love.

A small drop of matchmaker's advice

♡ One of the traditional skills I had to learn as a young man was building the drystone walls that divide the fields around the farm. They are hard to get just right. The stone we use here, which comes from Doolin and Liscannor, is smooth and so doesn't grip well; whereas the Burren stones have so many different little edges they stick to each other like glue. So working with Doolin stone it took a long time and a lot of practice to get at it and to persuade the stones to clinch together. Many was the time when we'd set the wall and then run like mad because we knew it would fall down before we were many yards away. And isn't a relationship just the same? One wrong stone, carelessly thrown in, and the whole thing crumbles. But if you take care and slowly build a solid foundation, it will resist the stiffest gust of wind. ♡

I knew that my matchmaking would happen in a very different environment from my father's and grandfather's. Their matchmaking had been conducted as business, though they did their best to find a match where love could grow in due course. By the time I started, young people were growing less happy about making a match only for land. They were moving forward and wanted more, wanted true love and passion. But to be honest they still didn't really know much about love and were anxious for any guidance, advice or connections I could make. That made life more difficult for me! There was no longer the logic my father and grandfather had been able to rely on. Now people wanted me to deliver the near-impossible, to look at a townful of potential partners and bring together the two people who were destined to feel passion for each other. They're still asking me, so I guess I must have risen to the challenge.

I set up shop as a matchmaker in the Irish Arms, a pub in Lisdoonvarna along the main street from the centre of the town. I was in the pub one day and your man the owner said, 'Look, Willie, you should use an old room in there as your office.' It was pretty informal. Lisdoonvarna is a small place, and it was quickly known that I could be found there.

An odd collection of people would come by this office. One I was very fond of was a tiny little woman in her sixties called Mary Beth. She was extremely religious, always carried a huge amount of prayer leaflets with her, and had scapular with pictures of Our Lord hanging around her neck and bracelets of miraculous medals around her wrists. Her face was permanently flushed from the anxiety she felt about all the carrying-on at Lisdoonvarna.

Mary Beth felt she was doing me a great service as she was in the way of telling everyone she met about me and then bringing them along to see me. She'd turn up with a number of potential customers for me and she was 100 per cent genuine and sincere in the interests of those people.

She brought in one fella this day and he was slow enough answering the usual questions I'd ask. Mary Beth had spent enough time in the office with me to know what my opening questions were, and so she started joining in, asking him too, 'Where do you live? And are you a farmer?' This particular man was a fella who was very fond of drinking and a bit of an old character, so when she asked him, 'What kind of a woman would you be looking for?' he says:

'Ah I don't mind, as long as she has a big arse and bigger tits.' Mary Beth practically fainted with the shock. She got down on her knees straight away and started saying prayers for him.

In these early days I felt it was great having Mary Beth around; she looked like a little saint with all her holy paraphernalia. I would always have a few posters up in the room, the odd motor-car calendar someone had given me, photos of women with not too many clothes on, a bit of fun in the midst of the serious stuff, a little bit provocative for fellas who were slow-moving. This is what I've always tried to do in my Lisdoonvarna matchmaking, add some fun to proceedings. So alongside all of these photos Mary Beth started putting up her own holy pictures to counteract their bad influence.

I got on so well with Mary Beth and she was very fond of me. I felt I wanted to protect her because I knew she could never tell if the fellas who were coming to see me were genuine or just little blaggards. Some of the men coming in felt very comfortable with her, and I'd nearly feel sorry that I had these pictures of naked women up on the walls, almost undoing the sincerity of it.

But most of the fellas she brought to me would be real scoundrels. Mary Beth thought she was helping them by finding a wife so they could settle down into holy matrimony, and believed this might save them from the demon drink. She didn't understand their true intentions: as one of them once said when he stepped into my office and saw all of Mary Beth's religious bits and pieces, 'This is like going on a pilgrimage to Knock. All I want is a woman for the night!'

One year Mary Beth stopped coming to Lisdoonvarna. I think a few of these lads had been rude to her and said some hurtful things, and she never came back. I missed her. Not that she was going to change anyone in Lisdoonvarna from their attitudes or ways, because it was a total town of drinking, always was and still is, but she added to the colour of everything.

Another visitor in those early days was a lovely boy called Larry Joe. He was a farmer on the Galway side of Lisdoonvarna, maybe thirty-six or so, tall and thinnish, red-haired, a right little gentleman and a very genuine person.

Larry Joe had a small enough farm which was very rundown: he had sold almost all his cows until he only had one left. Things were kind of bad. He almost had nothing to do so he'd spend a lot of time in with me, fetching drink for me, this and that, just marvellous. He had been quite a heavy drinker in the past but had stopped, so the office was handy, being just a bit off the line of fire from the temptations of the bar. Like Mary Beth he was an essential part of things, just as company.

One evening this lovely woman came in, very precise, very direct in what she said. Her directness was quite unusual. 'I joined the convent when I was sixteen, and was there for a considerable amount of time,' she said. 'But now I've been out for a while and I'd like to meet a partner. I don't want to spend the rest of my life alone.' Her name was Bernadette, and she must have been thirty or so now. As I was talking to her, Larry Joe popped his head in and said, 'Willie, I'll come back again. I'm just going to go down to the Ritz. Larry McEvoy is playing there, I'll go down and listen to him and I'll call up to you again.'

'Make sure you do,' I said.

As Bernadette and I were talking about the type of fellas I might have in the files, she said, 'What about that man going out, is he one of your customers?'

I did say, 'He is now,' even though Larry Joe had never said anything to me, not in too many words. I said, 'He's gone down to the Ritz' – this was about eight o'clock of a Friday – 'so why don't you come back in about nine-thirty and I'll have him here.' Somebody came in and I asked them to look after the office for a few minutes, as I wasn't far from the Ritz. There were always plenty of people who would man the desk if I needed to nip out.

I went over to the Ritz and found Larry Joe. 'Do you remember that girl when you were walking out, Larry?'

'Jeez, yes,' he said, 'she's a lovely girl.'

'Would you like to be introduced to her, just introduced, no big deal?'

'God,' he says, 'she looked nice.'

Back he came promptly at 9.30, so I introduced him to Bernadette. I was finishing up anyway so I went back down with the two of them, all three of us walked back to the Ritz. We talked away for a while and then she says to him, 'Can you dance?'

'I never did much of it,' he says. 'But come on, we'll tear out.'

Larry Joe was a big young fellow; he had a shabby jumper on him – not too new and the sleeves were shrunk – but he had a lovely face. They went out, had their waltz, and then Bernadette said she'd love to hear some traditional music. We went over to the Roadside Tavern, I think Ted Furey was there and some of his sons on that particular occasion. As usual a great session was going on. As we arrived I was teasing Bernadette for having been a nun, and suggested that we say one decade of the rosary. Larry Joe didn't realise I was messing and said, 'That's a good idea,' and started taking out his beads.

Bernadette was quicker with her reply, though. 'No,' she said, 'forget the rosary. I'll have another ball of malt.' As I went to get her the whiskey, I thought it seemed like she had definitely had enough of her years in the nunnery. After an hour I left them to themselves.

Bernadette and Larry Joe went on to get married. She was from out of the county, from Sligo or Roscommon, and they bought a little business up there, a shop, and were very happy together. That was a lovely outcome from the very early days of my matchmaking. I looked on it as a particularly good omen.

6
A Marriageable Age

Can a matchmaker make his own match? Everybody I meet seems to feel obliged, sooner or later, to ask me whether I arranged the match with my wife. Well, in a way I did, but I'm glad to say it was my father who finally made the marriage come about by planting the idea into my future wife Marie's head one day, although I guess both of us had been thinking about it.

My father had tried to marry me off at least once before. When I was eighteen or so he'd had his eye on one particular girl for me. What especially interested him was that she would bring to the marriage quite a lot of land, but at the age of eighteen the notion of owning land didn't impress me too much. That was a sign of the huge shift in attitudes to marriage that had taken place between our two generations.

I was not ready to get married. I was meeting an awful amount of girls, my social scene was fast-moving. It was very difficult for me to take the decision to stop the carousel and get married. All the time I kept saying, 'Jesus, I enjoy being free, I can't give this up yet.'

I fell in love with a lot of girls but I never settled. In my mind I always thought, Maybe there's another gorgeous girl just around the next turn of the road. And there nearly always was. I'd be meeting a beautiful girl one week, and have great feelings for her, but the following week I'd meet another girl. It isn't everyone would complain about that, of course. It took a long time for me to reach the point where I could see this way of life as terrible false, but when it did come the realisation was sudden. It completely turned me around. I didn't think I could have survived another year, carrying on the way I was – that's exactly how I felt: it was too much. I was drinking a lot and spending money very foolishly too. I think if I had gone even one more year I would have cracked up.

I had spent an awful amount of time either being in love or dreaming about love, one or the other, and sometimes, if I met someone very special, it was a little annoying that things didn't stay that way a little bit longer. But perhaps all those years of different relationships helped me later on as a matchmaker in the way of understanding things. I think it made me be very tolerant. When people say to me, especially if they have been hurt by going through a difficult separation, 'I won't make that mistake again,' I say, 'Maybe you should see whether the outcome might be different this time. No two situations are going to be the same.' I hate it when people turn so bitter and cold and imagine they will never be able to love again. As James Bond and I both agree, 'Never say never again.'

And it might come to what I constantly say to people, that it is very important to get married. I always stress that somewhere before you get too long in the tooth, if you can, allow yourself to marry and stabilise yourself and, if you want to, have children. To reassure people who are a bit nervous about the whole idea, I remind them that a very high percentage of marriages, in Ireland at least, work out. Look at the very worst that's going to happen, that you end up getting separated; if in the period of time that you're married, whether that's five years or twenty-five years, you have one or two children or however many, won't you actually have ended up with a lot to be thankful for?

There's an old story about the difficulties of finding a marriage. It's about the day St Bridget asked St Patrick to marry her. Just after dawn one day, St Bridget was taking a walk round Lough Neagh, up there in the north of Ireland, and lo and behold she bumped into St Patrick, as Irish saints were wont to do at the time. 'Good morning to you, Patrick,' says she. 'I'm very glad to see you today. I need to talk to you on a matter of some urgency.'

'Go ahead, Bridget,' Patrick replied. 'What is it that could be so important all of a sudden?'

'Well, the problem is that my nuns have been complaining they simply can't find a decent man to ask for their hand in marriage.'

Now what you have to understand is that at the time the nuns were not obliged to stay unmarried. Celibacy was a lifestyle choice, as we might say today. And those nuns in St Bridget's nunnery were getting more than a touch frustrated because none of the local men, all of them shy farmers and short of a few of the basic social skills, were willing to come forward and offer themselves as good husband material.

So Bridget looked Patrick in the eye. 'Here's my proposal. We women aren't allowed to ask men to marry us. But will you grant us the right to do that, so we can take the load off those clumsy, tongue-tied fellows worrying themselves to a frazzle?'

'Here's what I suggest,' said St Patrick. 'Once every seven years, since seven is a marvellous lucky number, I will give women the chance to ask a man for his hand in marriage.'

'One in seven?' spluttered Bridget. 'I'll be a wizened husk and ready for my grave by the time I have a chance to find a mate. You'll have to do better than that.'

'All right, I'll make it one year in four, but that's my final offer.'

Bridget pondered this for a while, and then accepted old Paddy's deal. 'But only if we start this year, right now.'

'That's perfectly fine with me,' said St Patrick.

'In that case, will you marry me, Patrick?'

'I can't, I'm a saint!' he said, chuckling merrily, and off he tripped along the shore of the lake.

So if even a saint like Bridget couldn't manage to find a marriage partner, it must be doubly difficult for us mere mortals!

I was in my very late twenties, twenty-eight in fact, before I met Marie. I had once had a few words of advice from an old man who told me, 'Willie, when the right person comes along, you'll know.' I took him at his word, and it was true.

I was in a pub in Ennistymon one night, out with a blonde-haired English girl I was seeing at the time; we were getting along grand. At one moment I looked up to see a girl with really beautiful blue eyes sit down near us and I thought, Jesus, that's the woman I'd like to marry.

A week passed. I was coming in one evening from saving hay and this same girl was riding out with a friend on the horses. There I was in a somewhat precarious predicament on my bicycle, holding the rake and a fork in one hand and steering with the other. Her horse went up to one side with the rattling of the bicycle, bumped into me and knocked me off. She fell off her horse and there we were, both sprawled on the ground. I looked into her eyes and I said to myself again, What a gorgeous woman. Literally falling in love!

Marie and I started dating after a while, and she got to

know my parents. My father had never said much, of course. He was an amazingly quiet kind of man. And at this stage of his life he was pretty well bedridden. He still religiously smoked a pipe, but that and a cup of tea were almost his only sustenance, as whenever he took a meal he hardly ate a thing. He had a small dog called Pip in his room, and when the food came he used to throw most of it to the dog. He lived on tea and tobacco for a long, long time.

The filling of the pipe was an important ritual for him. One day I went out somewhere and Marie stayed back in the house, alone apart from my father. He kept knocking on the floor and asking if there was anybody there who could fill his pipe. Marie went in to help him and they got chatting. She went into the kitchen to brew some tea and as she was going out of the door he said to her, casually it seemed, 'Would you ever have thought of marrying Willie?' She answered back from the kitchen, 'Yes, I would,' or something to that effect, so he called her back into his room again and they sat there for a while talking about marriage in general. That was typical of my father's subtle way of matchmaking – nothing too forceful, a word here, a suggestion there, just a flick of the reins, if you like, to guide a potential relationship onwards, giving it room to grow.

And that was that. My father died shortly afterwards, maybe only a month later. It was his final match. And Marie and I got married no more than three months after my father was laid to rest in the cemetery at Kilshanny.

A small drop of matchmaker's advice

♡ My father was a matchmaker of course, but so was my mother when it struck her. It was not unheard of for her to throw a casual observation to my sister about the good looks of a man who might be helping my father with the harvest. She might even go so far as to say, 'Jesus, if I wasn't married myself. . .' Of course it's only natural for a parent to want the best for their children, which is why they may try to steer them towards partners who they feel are a proper match. They all have their own schemes for matchmaking; my mother was a bit more obvious than my father. I think it can be very helpful, and at least entertaining, to give their advice more than a little thought. ♡

Marie and I were married in the spring, a traditional time of course, especially in these parts, where there would be a flurry of weddings around Shrove Tuesday. A boy and a girl from the town might have been going out for a long time and maybe they wouldn't have thought a lot at all about marriage. The fella mightn't have anyway, he might be happy enough with the situation. But then all of a sudden, the girl would be thinking, Well, Mary Malone down the road, she's getting married, and, John, we'll beat them to it then. The women would create a little race for the fellas and next thing they'd find themselves going over the line, willing or not!

The day Marie and I came back to Ballingaddy after our wedding, which was over in her parish in Limerick, we were visited in this old house by the strawboys. The strawboys are an age-old tradition in County Clare that I'm glad to say still exists; it's a *pishogue*, one of those supernatural rites and practices that have their roots in ancient Irish lore.

The strawboys are local folk who disguise themselves by dressing up in costumes made from straw, and turn up at the wedding celebrations. Now it would be in your interests that they'd come to you that night. It's supposedly very lucky for you if they do come, and a little bit unlucky if either they don't come or if you don't let them into the house.

The idea is that when they turn up they are very dressed up and their identity well concealed, so that the people inside the house won't recognise them. I'd always be a little canny and keep my eye on the strawboys' hands, because I found I could recognise them from that, and once they started dancing I'd know many of them by their dance steps, because over the years I have been one of those strawboys many times. When I was growing up they were very plentiful. And they still ask me now and again.

Imagine the scene in a farmhouse on the evening of a couple's wedding day. Most everyone would be in a grand good mood. The groom's mother might in reality be about to turn into a real demon of a mother-in-law, but even she'd be in good spirits that night because her son had got himself a bride, and she could see the possibility of an heir to the throne if you like. But oftentimes beneath the smiles she would be desperately jealous towards the new wife. Oh, there'd be an awful lot of jealousy in the house. All of a sudden it was like an old car being replaced with a new one. The mother-in-law could see that she was about to be left aside, that her position of power was under threat, but she would fight her redundancy very hard and be a very devil. Not in all cases, mind you, but more often than not. The old saying is that more than one woman in a kitchen is a recipe for disaster.

At any rate she'd be happy as Larry that evening, going around giving out teas, and everyone would be waiting for the strawboys to arrive. First the musicians would come. There'd always be good music, fiddles and accordions, something noisy and loud. And then from half-past ten onwards the strawboys would turn up.

You knew the minute they'd come in because they would be pounding on the floor with great sticks, a terrible belting on the floor, just for fun. That was my role as a boy, because I was too young for anything else. I'd have the pole and bang away, hammering it on the floor so that the crowd would scatter away back to make space for the strawboys.

My first outing as a strawboy was when I was about eleven. I went into a house with an older group of boys. That night we had to queue up for an hour and a half before getting inside, there were that many sets of strawboys. There might be six or seven sets of strawboys coming through in the one night.

Now one great sport for the fellas at these parties, especially the drunker ones, was to try and pull off the strawboys' masks – we call them eye fiddles, after the Irish word for them. They would be very curious to know who the strawboys were. And everyone would know you if they saw you, but the bit of mystery was they had to keep guessing. There was one man at this party, not a close relative, but a good friend of the family, and I knew him as well. And this little man kept picking at my eye fiddle all the time, pulling it, and eventually he brought it off so I had to use one hand to hold it up in front of my face. In truth it didn't really matter if I was seen, but being my first time, and still shy, I thought it would be the end of the world if my identity was revealed. I was very fond of this fella, but he was really bugging me.

At this time many houses had big old tea chests in the main room. They'd either be full of turf for the hearth, or have been emptied out and used for keeping babies in, like a wooden playpen. I remember we'd finished our turn and were on the way out, and this little man went for my eye fiddle one more time. I gave him a great push and over he tipped into a tea chest. All I could see were his two legs sticking up out of the chest. I wondered if I would get into trouble, but nobody else much noticed, since they were all busy watching the footwork of the dancers, and as I was leaving I could see the little man himself laughing as he got back up.

There were different motivations for joining in with the strawboys. Often it was for the dancing. Generally the women who join in with the strawboys dress up as men, and the fellas as women, so when it comes to the dancing a man may decide to dance as the woman, though it's not easy. I've also often danced as a woman with another fella, and where two men dance together it's known as a 'buck set'.

The second reason there were so many strawboys was because you'd get a free drink for your troubles. It was marvellous in a sense. The family would bring a white enamel bucket of porter to you outside. You couldn't stay in the house after dancing; you'd come out and go into a shed near the house, with maybe a little light from candles placed in scooped-out turnips, which were safer than using glass jars near hay because the turnips would still be moist. They'd bring out the bucket of porter and give you jampots to drink out of. They probably wouldn't have the cups to spare, or they'd be afraid you'd break the cups or glasses anyway.

The second night we went to be strawboys we were getting more cheeky, so we tried to go in twice for another round of drinks. We came out, changed our clothes around a little bit and turned up again, but the man of the house recognised us and they hunted us out.

There'd be many strawboys in elaborate costumes that

were awfully well done, a hat like a crown with four prongs coming up off it into a point with a ball on top. But most times as youngsters we just stuck straw into our normal clothes. On my first attempt we went to this old farmer we knew and he told us, 'Go up to the hay shed, there's straw there.' We stuffed it around us but it wasn't held tight. By the time we'd banged the poles and danced some sets, Jesus, the house would be saturated with straw. No wonder some of the new brides wouldn't want the strawboys in their new house.

The tradition is not so common now, although it carries on in the hotels, in a more organised way, for wedding parties, more of a performance and more impersonal, but you can still have great fun. The last time I went I danced like hell, and I don't think anyone recognised me . . .

Now whether as a strawboy or an invited guest, I have attended many marriage celebrations over the years, many of which I had a hand in bringing about, but one of the strangest was the wedding of Donal Dan Paddy, Stephen and Murt.

I was at the October horse fair in Kilrush town when three men I had known for a while approached me. 'Willie,' they said, 'we want to marry a wife.' I looked at them, and thought, That is a relief, for whatever my chances of getting one wife, it would be a miracle to find three wives, as they were quite old and unattended to.

They were three brothers, but each was totally different from the others. Donal Dan Paddy was the oldest and the spokesman for the trio. He was the roughest-looking man I think I ever saw. Tall and broad with a huge head and strong face, the only hair he had was coming out in great grey tufts from his nose and ears. His nickname was Dusty, because whenever he got a slap on the back or shoulder a white cloud would rise up. This, I thought, was because instead of hanging up his coat in the evenings he would throw it on the sack of flour that was in every Irish home at that time.

His brother Stephen could have been a film star. He was also tall, but slim, elegant and very handsome, a little like Gregory Peck. Yet he was strong. Once I heard it said that a herd of cattle had rushed through the farm and he caught and held a three-year-old bull by the horns. It would take a giant of a man to do this.

Murt, the third brother, on the other hand was small, stout, exceedingly happy and humorous. Quickly I said to myself, What a pity the tradition is to leave the family farm to the oldest son, as it won't make my own work easier. Either Stephen or Murt would be much easier to find a partner for.

I arranged to meet the brothers in one of the pubs later. I was busy selling horses and afterwards I bought a beautiful cream-coloured palomino pony from a man in west Clare; his daughter Annie was holding the pony still. The pony wasn't young, the man had had her a long time and it was with a lot of reluctance he eventually agreed to let me have the pony. Their biggest fear was that I was an agent, buying horses for the factory, to be killed for meat, and they didn't want the pony to suffer that fate.

I introduced myself as Willie Daly from Ennistymon and told him that I was opening a riding school and wanted the pony for children. His daughter said she had heard of Willie Daly, and wasn't I the matchmaker? At this her father became more willing to part with the pony and also mentioned that he had another old one at home, which I eventually bought. As we were concluding the deal he quietly asked me whether I could find a partner for his daughter. 'She's a lovely girl,' he said, 'very good around the house, able to cook a dinner and bake bread, milk and feed cows.' I knew it would be easy to find a partner for her; I said we'd talk more about this when I was collecting the other pony.

Later on in the evening I again met Dusty, Stephen and Murt. They worked very hard and were not often in the pubs; in their own way they looked more superior than anyone else there. They seemed to have found a new happiness, perhaps in the thought that they would have a new woman in their house. It was as if this thought never occurred to them before and now it was the most prominent thing in their minds. As I walked into the pub the three of them approached me. 'Willie, did you have any luck at the fair for us?'

I didn't want to seem too enthusiastic but yet did not want to dash their new-found hope. I felt a little sad as I was unsure that I could do anything for them since they had left it a little late in life. I told them about meeting a lovely girl called Annie with red hair, blue eyes and freckles. Murt was the first to react, with a twinkle in his eye. He said, 'She'll do grand – we'll marry her!' I couldn't help but laugh at his excited reply, but it made me think that perhaps I had judged the situation wrong and that maybe it had not yet been decided which of the three brothers would marry.

Even though I was tired at the end of a long day at the horse fair, their energy was contagious. Somebody said, 'Willie, sing a song.' I always liked to start the ball rolling and so I sang a great song called 'The German Clockwinder'. The song tells the story of a Dublin housewife whose husband is away and who is visited by the blond German clockwinder of the title, one Benjilum Fooks. Her husband comes back just as Benjilum is busy 'winding her clock'.

> *The husband says he, 'Now look here, Mary Jane,*
> *Don't let that blond German in here again.*
> *He wound up your clock and left mine on the shelf.*
> *If your old clock needs winding, sure I'll wind it myself!*
> *With your tool-a-lumma, tool-a-lumma, tool-lil-i-ay!'*

This started a little session and then the gramophone was taken down and a record of the Kilfenora Ceili Band was put on. The woman behind the bar came out to give Dusty the kitchen broom. A great roar went up from the crowd. 'C'mon, Dusty, c'mon, Dusty!' I had no idea what was going to happen. Eventually and slowly Dusty took off his old flour-covered coat and threw it on the ground; the crowd opened a good-sized space for him, still cheering. He held the brush in his right hand and to every beat of the tune he swapped it from right to left, and moved his right and left leg over the handle of the brush. Then he dropped it to the ground, dancing over and around the handle. His agility and footwork simply amazed me.

Before I left I told the brothers that there would be a horse fair in Ennistymon at the end of that November and could they make it there? They said they would and I promised that I'd see if I could get Annie to come. As I said my goodbyes Murt followed me outside and insisted on putting a pound note into my pocket. This confused me more about which one was to get married, but he insisted on me taking the money.

In the meantime I visited Annie's house to collect the other pony and to discuss a possible match. I told her father about the brothers. He wanted to know practical details, like how many acres of land they had, how many chains there were in the cow house – as it was common for people to borrow cows so they would look more prosperous and get a bigger dowry. Was the house thatched or slated, did they have a hay shed, did they have bog? The next question he asked, which I had never been asked before, was whether there were thistles on the land. Later I asked an old man about the thistle question and he answered, 'Sure they only grow on good land.'

Annie's father then told me what her dowry would be: a brood mare and two young milking cows. As they had no relations in America to send home money for the purpose of a dowry, no money would change hands. Annie's thoughts were far from these practical matters as she piped up suddenly to ask, 'Is he good-looking?'

I thought for a moment, as this was difficult to answer since I still wasn't sure which of the brothers was the one who might marry her. My answer must have sounded funny to her. 'They are,' I said.

The day of the horse fair at Ennistymon arrived. Mid-morning Dusty and his two brothers came by with a horse and jaunting car and three horses tied behind. They passed by and acknowledged me before taking a place in the fair not far from where I was. Some hours passed. Just after midday Annie, her father and a family friend arrived. They came up to me and we talked. I was in the middle of a deal so I just asked if they could ramble back to me in a short while. Half an hour passed and the question on my mind as I saw them approach was, Which of the brothers am I going to introduce them to? Annie looked lovely in a bright yellow costume, slim and young and full of life – she stood out at the fair. We talked for a minute and I could see her looking around, wondering was it this fella, was it that fella?

After a few moments of trying to work out how in the name of God I could do this and which of the brothers I ought to start with, we walked over to meet them. Dusty was the nearest, so I introduced him to Annie first. As she looked at him I could see the disappointment flash across her face and then she said, 'Willie, I'm leaving', and turned away to walk down by Marrinan's pub. I felt bad as I watched her hurry away, and wondered what I thought I was doing.

The footpaths there were of very uneven flags, with lots of steps, and all covered with horse and cow dung. Annie slipped and fell close to Cullinan's pub, a right good fall, and she must have banged her head, as she made no effort to get up. A number of people gathered around to assist her. Stephen came down with me, gently picked her up and placed her in the trap. An old lady had some smelling salts and as Annie came around Stephen was cleaning off her costume, covering her with a rug and putting hay around her feet to keep her warm. She looked up at him and with a smile on her face asked whether he was the man that she was going to marry. Stephen said he was and sat in beside her where they spoke for a while.

I headed back down to where Dusty and Murt were. I think Dusty knew what I was going to tell him, as before I could say anything he said, 'She has no interest in me, Willie, but it would be great if she has in Stephen.' I walked back over to Stephen and Annie and suggested that we all go into Cullinan's for a drink. Stephen took Annie by the hand and said to me, 'We'll join you in five minutes.' They went into Paddy Twomey's draper shop, where Stephen bought her a new dress to replace her torn, dirty one. As

7
Into My Stride

By the time I married Marie I had been at the matchmaking for nearly four years, so she only ever knew me as a matchmaker. Strangely enough, through all the years of it, Marie never put any great emphasis on what I did. She seemed to understand without asking what I had to do, and would be very good whenever people visited the house to look for me.

Although she might come with me a few times to Lisdoonvarna every year, she never got to attend an awful lot of what was going on, because we had a good number of children and quite quickly, and she was always minding the house. While we were in the middle of raising our family, I did try to wind down my level of activity. When you have children, your priorities naturally change, and I enjoyed being with them at home as well. But it would never be long before there was someone else knocking at the door.

A lot of people in Ireland would be aware of Lisdoonvarna and the Matchmaking Festival, but they did not always realise that the festival lasted for over a month, and some seemed not even to know it began in September, as they would come to find me in March or May and ask where the festival was. It was mainly men who visited the house. There'd be the odd exception when the Matchmaking Festival was on that a group of women would drive over in a car, in which case Marie would be very hospitable, bring them in, and they'd all have a great laugh together.

She was very courteous with these people, no matter what they'd be or who they'd be. They'd come to our door and she'd be as nice as pie: 'Come in, Willie's just over in the yard there.' Marie was very young-looking and sometimes the visitors would ask her, 'Is that your father over there?' She'd enjoy a quiet chuckle as she put the tea on. I must have looked a bit older even when I was young; I had the white hair even then, and a beard. I had started wearing a beard quite young, at eighteen or nineteen. We had to shave by candlelight as there was no electricity, which always cast a shadow. The blades were very bad, like using a blunt bread-knife. There was only one mirror in the wardrobe door and most of the silver had fallen off that. Since I had a very dark heavy beard, shaving was impossible. When I'd get out in public I'd find I'd missed half of the beard, so in the end I thought, To hell with that, and let my beard grow.

But there were a handful of occasions when I cut the beard

off. And one of these times I headed down to the Roadside Tavern for a few pints with Patsy Whelan and Ted Furey. There was a lovely guy from Liscannor, Jimmy McDonough, who also frequented the Roadside. We'd sit and talk about horses and farming and listen to the music. Well, I'd had my beard cut for three or four days. I walked in to the Roadside, turned to Jimmy and said, 'How are you?'

'I'm good,' he answered, but rather curtly.

'What are you drinking?' I asked him.

'I'm OK.' He turned round and looked at me. 'Where are you from?'

'Kilshanny,' I said.

'Oh, I know a fellow from there,' said Jimmy. 'He's called Willie Daly.'

'I *am* Willie Daly!'

We laughed. Then I saluted Patsy and Ted, who were playing some music, and there was no salute back. No reaction at all. I must have looked very different. When Patsy and Ted realised it was me, they really couldn't believe it. So if I'm ever forced to go on the run, all I'll need to do is cut my beard, I'll be fine.

I started to get a small amount of publicity. Each year some newspaper or other would come down to Lisdoonvarna and write an article about me. For many years we hadn't had a phone at the house so if journalists came to Clare they just sort of hit into town to see if I was there, and if I wasn't in the Lisdoonvarna office they might track me down to Ballingaddy.

It was all quite low-key, but gradually word about me spread beyond Ennistymon, Lisdoonvarna and out from County Clare. One year I got some national press coverage as 'Ireland's youngest matchmaker', so of course more and more people came looking for me. There was a handful of radio interviews, occasionally even a little bit of television, a flurry of activity, and then things would calm down for the next eleven months.

Come the next September, I would open up my 'office' again. After three seasons in the Irish Arms, the owner of the Hydro Hotel – which is at the other end of the main street in Lisdoonvarna but closer to the centre of things – asked whether I would consider doing something over at his place. So I moved over to a new room just off the reception area. And just as at the Irish Arms, I never knew who would come walking through that door. Once in a while an odd fella would be pushed in. A group of eight or nine men would turn up and they'd always have some little character with them, a mad little fella that they'd want to get in to see what his reactions would be. That's typical of Lisdoonvarna.

And of course I'd be ready for that. There was this one little lad, Din Din, who would be bundled in regular every year. He was small, about four foot eight, and looked immaculate on the Friday night, with a lovely blue pinstripe suit, white shirt and tie, his hair neatly combed back – he hadn't much hair on one side but he'd bring it across from the other – and a very amusing face. I would hear a commotion outside the office, the thrust from outside the door and he'd tumble inside. None of the fellas with him seemed to show their own face, though.

Din Din would end up in front of me, both hands in his pockets, and swagger around the room a bit, a massive smile on his face. 'Can you get me a woman?'

'Sure we'll see if we can, like.'

So we'd sit him down and I'd say, 'Now, what kind of woman do you want?'

And he'd always answer the same way: 'I want a tall one.' He was definitely a bit strange, and never seemed to make a go of it with any of the women I introduced him to.

I used to feel a little sorry for him, because he'd start off all optimistic at the beginning of the weekend, but as the nights wore on he grew more and more depressed and by Sunday he'd be awful low, drinking a lot, and his shirt and suit rumpled and stained. One night he told me, 'Jesus, if I don't get a woman tonight I'm going to commit suicide.'

'Don't go doing that,' I said, keeping my tone light, 'because you might only just have that done and she might come the next few days after. You can't get a woman like a parcel, coming in the post. It takes a little while, but they do come and you will get one.'

Eventually one night this big, tall woman called Colette came in – she was with two friends. When I asked her about her tastes in men, she replied, 'I don't mind what he looks like, as long as he's a good sense of humour.' I immediately thought of little Din Din:

'There's a fella there, he's very good fun. I've known him for a little while, you should meet him.'

I introduced Din Din to Colette at one of the Lisdoonvarna venues. The first thing she asked him was 'Can you dance?' There was good rock 'n' roll music that night. Din Din just looked up at her as she towered over him, and nodded his head to say that he could. I also brought one of her friends out for a dance, something I'd often do as it would kick in a bit of interest. Out we all went on the floor and I glanced across to see how Colette and Din Din were getting along.

My God, this lad, he was great entertainment. Colette was a good five foot ten, maybe more, and he was going all around her, dancing and hopping up off the ground to get his hands around her. She was not a great dancer, but anxious to learn and mad to dance – she had a big long stride, and was stepping on his feet at times. That's probably why he was hopping so much. At one point they were jiving to the music, but despite their height difference he somehow managed to swing her right under his hands. There was the odd collision, of course, but they were both laughing. At the end of the song she grabbed him for a finish off the floor and swung him in her arms four or five times around. She was obviously loving it. A little later on, during a second dance, I could see he had jumped up on her back like a jockey. They were having so much fun.

I saw them once again together that weekend, and then never again much after that though, which I felt was a shame.

Din Din came back in the office again a few years later. He seemed to have grown a little bit older in himself, a little bit quieter. His opening line was the same, though: 'Can you get me a woman?' I was tempted to say, 'What did you do with that lovely big tall Colette I found for you, then?', but I said nothing. There was no point in making him feel worse about it.

Even when things didn't work out, I always thrived on the contact with people. During the festival I found it was usually better to get things moving on the very night someone came to see me, because if it was, say, a Friday night when they came in and were intent on meeting someone, if I left it to the following night they might be hard to find again. Mainly I'd say to people that would come in at half-seven, because generally speaking half-seven up to nine is relatively quiet, 'Look in again later on.' They might come in again too soon, after less than an hour, and there might still be no change. The spark would not yet have come into the night. So I'd tell them, just as I still do, 'OK, go back down to Rathbaun's or the Ritz, or across to the Royal Spa or the Roadside Tavern, and when you're passing back again look by, but make sure you *do* come back.' The trick was to keep them busy while I could try and find the fella or the girl I had in mind for them.

Between a fella's first time coming and the third time, a girl might have come in who would have suited him, and then they'd be gone. So I might then say, 'You come back at half-ten or eleven o'clock and I'll have the girl with me here,' and I'd go off and find her and make sure she was in the vicinity at the right time. That would be grand; we'd go into the reception area and I'd catch the girl by the hand and bring her up through the crowd.

I used to do everything by memory. As I've got a little older, I might have to write their names down on my hand, but I still have very vivid pictures of their faces, and even though there are so many matches during the festival it normally works quite well. I'd be awfully surprised when I'm walking down the street and somebody would shout across, 'How are you, Willie? How's this and that? Do you remember you introduced us five years ago?' I mightn't quite remember that. But I'd have to say I do, of course.

Of course, I do have the ledger handed down from my grandfather and father, which I still use to make a record of all the men and women who ask me to make a match. Although much of what I do relies on my instinct and my gut feeling, I also make detailed notes about their age – I always make a polite guess for the women – marital status, appearance, jobs and personality. I ask them for their personal preferences for a partner. And those notes are about as scientific as it gets. The real analysis goes on in my brain, in my soul, as I think about two people I have come across separately and imagine them spending time together.

The one great advantage of being in the office during the festival is that I have met, seen and talked to everybody I am trying to make a match for. When I am matchmaking for people who have written to me for help, I have to be extra careful. The rest of the year, outside the festival time, I don't ask for photographs, though sometimes people send them in, assuming I do. I like to preserve a sense of anticipation. As I always say, it's nice to have the element of surprise. And as one girl said to me, it could be a shock as well.

Aileen was a farmer's daughter of about twenty-eight, very quietly spoken, good-looking and with a nice enough job. I put her in touch with a man called Davey who had contacted me by mail, and they started writing to each other. She was from the Galway side; he was from Limerick. They had grown very close. On three occasions they tried to meet but somehow they missed each other, or one of them had to cancel at the last moment. So I decided to help and fixed for both of them to meet me at the Lady Gregory Hotel in Galway. I went to meet Aileen beforehand elsewhere in the town and by the time we drove over to the hotel we were late for the appointed time.

There were only a few people in the hotel bar, an old woman at one of the tables, across from her a young girl doing her lessons, another woman of about forty-five or fifty, and an old man sitting up at the bar. Aileen and I had a drink, and she told me Davey had sent her his photograph. I took a quick look, as I had never met him, and went up to the barmaid and asked her, 'Have you seen any tall, dark-haired young men in here in the last hour?'

'Since we've opened this is all that's been here,' she said, so I thought we must have missed him.

I went back to sit at the table and the old man at the bar came over. 'Are you Willie Daly?'

'I am.'

'Well, I am Davey.'

Aileen looked up at him, her drink up to her mouth, put her drink straight back down and went out the door without a word, leaving the photo behind.

He sat down with me and I said, 'You can't be surprised, Davey, that photo was very misleading.'

He thought for a while and said, 'She asked me for a photo a couple of weeks ago, and that was the only picture I ever got taken of myself.' It must have been from forty years before!

About nine or ten days passed. Aileen phoned me and said, 'Willie, I miss Davey's letters.'

'Do you, Aileen? That photograph Davey sent you was a genuine mistake. He didn't do it intentionally as much as you might have thought. Why don't you start writing to him again? He'd be too shy and embarrassed now to get back in touch with you, I'd say.'

They began writing to each other once more and, wonderfully, they ended up getting married and having a little baby. Davey died about a year or two after the baby was born, alas, but even in their far too short time together he and Aileen had known great happiness.

It was proof that if a flicker of magic is there you should never try and put too many impediments or prejudices in its way. But that's not a set and dried rule. There are times when I'll say, 'Don't rush in,' mainly if I have been approached by a woman who has been widowed or separated and has a number of children. I feel then that it is especially important that she finds the right man, with a good temperament, because she might quickly meet a man she likes but find out later that he's not nice to her children. That's one of the few times I would say, 'Take it easy, don't make that decision today, take your time.' But otherwise every occasion has its new possibilities, and everyone is entitled to a new chance.

A small drop of matchmaker's advice

♡ *I find both men and women often fall into habits when trying to find a match. I had been trying to help a lovely, redheaded woman a few years back. She was good-looking, early thirties and quite fiery. She insisted that she'd like a man who was like her – fun-loving and a bit loud – even though she'd had no luck with these fellas. I'd tell her I thought she should try a quieter man but she kept coming back to me looking for a hooley. Sadly, she's still looking because habit is a hard thing to break.*

If the grass out on the side of the road is very green and very sweet, when a cow starts breaking out on the road once, she's going to do it again even though there's perfectly green and sweet grass in the field where she is. A horse is the same. Once they get used to the nice bit of green grass, they'll come up for the same sweet picking, time and time again. But nevertheless I think people can and do change. It takes a lot of effort, though. Change is something you have to be always prepared to accept, that people will be different. It is very easy to get stuck in a rut by looking again and again for the same kind of person – and maybe the wrong kind of person. ♡

Sometimes it would take a dramatic turn of events to allow a couple to break out of the pattern of their lives.

One day I was out in the bog cutting turf. My bank of turf that day was out on the Ennistymon–Lisdoonvarna road. I used to travel to the bog on a pony and cart, and at the time I had a beautiful black and white pony. I tied him to the axle of the cart while I got on with the work. Everyone passing would take time to admire him. Some days busloads of tourists would drive by and stop to watch us cutting the turf. We would show them how and then let them have a go. At midday we would all gather round a good fire made from *caoráns* – small dry sods of turf or bogdale – heating kettles and saucepans of water to make tea or boil eggs, laughing and chatting.

One afternoon I saw a woman and a youngish man looking out at my pony. It turned out she, her husband and son had a bank of turf about fourteen miles away from the Carrig Mountains where we had our own turf. I offered them a cup of tea and she explained why she had come to find me. 'Our donkey fell into a bog hole last fall,' she said, 'and now we have no animal to put out our turf with and bring it home.' This was a problem, since they would need the turf for their fires that coming winter.

I told her, 'I know a man who has an ass.'

'Ah,' she said, 'that's great. Where is he then?'

I added that the ass was due to be a dowry to whoever married the man's daughter. She looked at her son and said, 'You'll marry her.' The boy seemed emotionless and said nothing.

I told them where the man, the girl and the ass lived. The mother wanted me to come too, so we arranged to meet there a day or so later. This time the mother brought her husband as well as her son.

The daughter, Noreen, was sweet and lovely. She tried talking straight away to the boy, who was called Jimmy Rua from his red hair, but he would not reply. The father hardly spoke either. They were both very dour. It was the mother who did all the talking. That's the way it was in some houses. She quickly got round to asking about the ass. She wanted to know whether the ass had been carred, in other words trained to pull a cart. Had it opened drills in the garden and pulled a plough? The answer to all her questions was yes. She looked at Jimmy Rua and seemed pleased.

We went up the side of a mountain to where there were three lovely green fields. It was like the oasis in the desert. Noreen's father told me as I admired them, 'It took all my years to make them look green as they are now. I carried everything up here: manure, seaweed.' He was bent and old. I somehow felt that he had achieved a lot. The image of those three lush fields and the barrenness of the countryside all around them still stays in my mind.

As we entered the first of the fields a big black ass rushed close to us, braying. Jimmy Rua's mother waited until he had quietened down a little, then went over to the ass and walked round him. She lifted his tail, then suddenly bent down and put her hand underneath him to feel if he was – how can I put this politely? – fully intact, since she probably guessed he looked like a jack. She straightened up and said, 'He's a full jack. He's no use to us for the turf – too bold, too uncontrollable.'

Noreen quickly said, 'It's not him. *She's* in the third field.' We went up there to see a lovely grey mare. Noreen walked over and put her arms about its neck. They looked a picture.

Jimmy Rua's mother checked the ass up and down, took off her headscarf to make a halter out of it and told Jimmy to get on the mare's back. 'Ask her to go forward, ask her to go back,' she told him. The donkey, like Jimmy, was obedient. And the mother said, 'She'll do.' The woman almost didn't look at Noreen. I said to myself, That old woman will kill Noreen when Jimmy Rua marries her. On the way back she said to me, 'We'll do this fast, as the turf will be ready to put out by mid-July. There is no time to waste.'

The match was quickly made. Jimmy Rua and his father still hadn't said a word.

The marriage was set for the eighth of August. Everyone seemed happy enough, as the weather was very fair and it was a good hot summer. Jimmy Rua's mother asked if I could arrange for her to get the dowry before the wedding. I told her that was a bit unusual; normally it was on the day of the wedding itself or the day after or so. She said, 'The bogs are very dry now. If it rains we won't get to travel as it will get too soft and we won't get to put out the turf.' She sent Jimmy with me to arrange this.

Noreen's father agreed: 'She's right about the ground being good now.' Noreen and Jimmy Rua went up the mountain to fetch the donkey. As they were coming down the mountain Jimmy was riding the donkey and Noreen up behind him with her arms about his waist. They laughed non-stop, as it's hard to stay on a donkey.

They went and put out the turf for the winter fire. Now, Jimmy's mother had the grazing of the grass of the local Protestant church and graveyard. She told Jimmy to put the ass in to eat the grass. The very next day they found the ass dead of a colic. There was war. Jimmy's mother got on to me and we visited Noreen's father. She gave out to him with a voice as cold as the wind off the mountains, 'There will be no wedding as that ass was wrong.' Noreen's father replied,

'Well, there was nothing wrong with that ass until you changed her religion!' And indeed the wedding never happened. I think Noreen's father was secretly pleased that his daughter would not have such a mother-in-law inflicted on her.

Later I heard that Jimmy and Noreen eloped on the other donkey, the big black jackass, rode all the way to Dublin and went to London, where they lived and raised a fine big family.

They had had to take drastic action to see their match through, and had believed strongly enough in the strength of their love to take the necessary risk. Stories like theirs made being a matchmaker worthwhile, creating love for those who were prepared to take the necessary leap of faith.

8
Try, Try Again

Whenever I was not actively matchmaking, I had plenty of other work to do, not least on the farm, which I was still running. Calling in the cattle, waiting overnight for a delicate mare to foal, reading the shifts in the weather, all the changing seasons and tasks of a farmer's life helped keep me down to earth after an interview on the television.

As the demands of the farm fluctuated through the year, so love followed its own patterns and seasons. There was always a big rush to get married before Shrove Tuesday as the next day, Ash Wednesday, marked the start of Lent and from then on no marriages were permitted until after Easter. The imminent arrival of Shrove Tuesday would encourage all manner of shenanigans, deviations and tricks as the women who were keen to tie the knot used their wiles to try and outwit their reluctant partners.

We saw a similar effect every Good Friday and Christmas Day, the only two days in the whole year when the pubs would close. And Jesus, people would panic. It didn't matter that the pubs could open for every one of the other 363 days: they had to have a drink that very day. In their desperation and anxiety they would be phoning the pub owners, knocking on their side doors and trying to persuade them to sneak them in. And then the next day, when the landlords could open up again, these men who had been so desperate the day before might not even go near the pub. It was exactly the same effect with the prospect of the ban on weddings during Lent.

A woman called Elly had been going out for the best part of twenty years with Paddy. She'd often drop him a hint about getting married, but always to no avail. On the anniversary of their twenty years together, Elly asked Paddy, 'Isn't it about time we got married?' but Paddy replied, 'But sure who'd marry either of us now?'

Now it just so happened that Paddy had had a long falling-out with his neighbour Jack over which of them owned the field where Paddy had been grazing his donkey for years (there were frequently disputes over land: I did once hear that maybe the reason Ballingaddy means 'home of the thief' was something to do with just that). So when Jack produced a clutch of maps showing that the field was in his portfolio of land, Paddy went mad. They ended up going to court to settle the issue, but Jack had it all in black and white.

Jack had also been seen out a lot with a nice young girl at Mass, in the town and shopping on market days. The rumour went out that Jack had got himself a girlfriend, and Elly quickly conveyed this message to Paddy, adding almost as an afterthought that she had heard Jack was going to the parochial house to see the priest and secure the last available slot for a wedding before Lent.

At that Paddy jumped up with anger and envy at Jack's good fortune. He called him every name under the sun, including land grabber and thief. Elly quickly seized the moment, saying, 'Well, Paddy, wouldn't it be great to beat him to it? Let's go to Father Tim right away and sneak that last space from under Jack's nose.' Paddy snatched up his coat, grabbed his bike and said, 'Come on, let's get going!' Elly jumped briskly on to the bar of the bike and they sped straight off to the priest's house, made the arrangements and got married on Shrove Tuesday.

A few weeks went past. Whenever Paddy crossed paths with Jack, he always put on his broadest smile. But it came to his attention that Jack was now always on his own. Although Paddy was desperate to gloat over his victory in getting the final wedding slot, he couldn't bring himself to ask Jack directly where his bride-to-be was, as he had sworn never to talk a single word to him ever again after the trouble over the field. But discreetly he made enquiries to find out about the girl who had been seen around and about with Jack. It turned out that she was none other than Jack's niece and that he occasionally accompanied her to church or into town as a favour to his widowed sister.

Over supper that evening Paddy mentioned this to Elly, who said, 'Oh, that's strange. I'm sure I heard it was Jack who was going to marry, but maybe they told me wrong.' And as she got up from the table and turned to go and fetch another plate of colcannon and stew from the stove, I do believe a slight smile played about her lips, though I could have heard that wrong too.

So sure, a commitment to romance can be forced if needs must, though, as I say, love is a year-round affair, whether the sleet is lashing in from the coast in January, the whitethorn blossom opening in May, the hay reeks rising high during August or the nights turning in early before Christmas.

And to be honest there is nothing amiss with giving love a helping hand. In the matchmaking you can sense that a couple will find great happiness together, but often one of them seems to be stubbornly resistant to the idea, and maybe needs a swift shove in the right direction to realise the error of his or her ways.

A little bit of craft can always come in handy. Do you know the story of the fox and the crow? One day a fox noticed a big block of cheese had been left outside. He was just about to pick it up and enjoy an unexpected snack when a crow swooped down, grabbed the cheese and flew off into the bushes. The fox struck up a conversation with the crow: 'What a lovely day, my dear, a beautiful day, isn't it?' But the crow was not responding; she wanted her cheese. The fox carried on: 'Why don't you sing me a song?' No reply, so the fox tried again. 'I believe most crows don't have a good voice, but I've heard that you have a marvellous singing voice, why don't you let me hear you?' By now the crow must have been getting a bit vain, I suppose, so she decided she would sing a song. The moment she opened her mouth the cheese fell out, and the wily old fox had won the day.

A small drop of matchmaker's advice

♡ *With cup of tea in hand, I instinctively check the weather first thing each morning: I have, after all, been a farmer for over fifty years. We all know that old adage 'red sky in the morning, shepherd's warning'. I feel you can read similar signs in love. But so many people ignore the little clues. We have a local phrase in Clare, 'the thin breeze', a subtle, soft breeze close to the ground, a sign of rain but one that is often missed. People often fail to spot the 'thin breeze' in a new relationship, a change in the climate that will tell you whether the prospects of a relationship may be sunny or stormy. Trust in the messages that nature, human nature, is sending you.* ♡

A young man approached me one day at the cattle mart. He told me his name was Kevin, that he was twenty-seven and that he was looking for a wife. Twice he said, 'I don't smoke and I don't drink.' I was tempted to say, 'That's a shame,' as my father always said a man smoking or taking a moderate drink could be a good sign of his temperament. 'Irish people should have great temperaments, then,' he'd go on, 'as they drink a lot. It makes people want to sing and dance – and only fight sometimes.'

Kevin and I spoke for a while about a girl I had in mind for him. He seemed to think he was quite a catch for a woman because he didn't smoke. He asked, 'Has she money or a job?' This was disappointing, because I would always hope younger people would look for love more than financial gain. Marrying for money was the old way of things.

The girl I had in mind was an extremely tall young woman called Dorothy who was perhaps ten years older than him, in her late thirties. I arranged for them to meet. Dorothy's father walked in front of her, and wasted no time introducing them. Kevin shook Dorothy's hand cautiously. Now, Kevin was barely five foot or so. Dorothy must have been over six foot tall: she towered above the lad. He said nothing. She held on to his hand with both of hers for what seemed a long time. Kevin took back his hand, turned, walked away and then ran. I turned to Dorothy and her father and could do nothing but apologise and turn my hands to the sky in disbelief.

'That's a shame,' Dorothy's father said, 'I had plenty to give with her.' He told me he had a picture of John F.

Kennedy and Jacqueline, and a statue of a hen and a clutch of chickens. I quietly said to myself, 'Well, that dowry has variety.' It reminded me of a song about a man whose daughter was six foot four inches in her stockings and quite broad, and it was proving hard to get a partner for her. The father was giving a good dowry for her – 'Ten silver sovereigns down I will pay you, A three-legged stool and a fine feather bed' – though not one statue of a hen and chickens.

I consoled Dorothy, and told her that there was no reason to be down-hearted. We would try, try again, but I was certain that we would only need the one more try. That same night I ran into a young man called PJ at Connor's pub in Doolin, where he always was of an evening and always half drunk. He'd grab my arm: 'Jesus, Willie, will you get me a wife? If she answers the rosary that will do me.' I liked PJ. He had a big head of curly red hair that looked as if he never combed it, and he wore green wellingtons which a goat must have eaten because there were great chunks missing out of them. PJ used to paint the hay barns when he wasn't in the pub, and always seemed to have a variety of colours on his hair, face and clothes – red, blue, green, yellow. It advertised his trade.

I told him about Dorothy and her disappointment, and described her height and width and said she was around his age. He said, 'She'll do grand.' When I told him her father was offering a dowry he couldn't believe it. That was a great match. As soon as PJ and Dorothy met, it felt as though they had been together for years. They married and had six lovely children. Dorothy was a great wife and mother. And whenever I asked her about PJ's drinking, she'd say to me, 'He needs some outlet, the poor creature. And besides,' she'd add, 'Guinness is a marvellous aphrodisiac also.'

So I never give up hope, and maybe because of that, when a match doesn't happen, the people involved keep coming back. There's a lovely fella from Corofin, Fergus, a farmer with slightly crooked eyes and a heart of gold. He's in his late forties, but he has never married. When he was in his twenties he fell in love with a local girl from Ennistymon who I had introduced him to. The girl's father didn't want her to marry a farmer, but they became secretly engaged and made plans to run away to Dublin. However, her family heard about it, and they stepped in to stop the elopement. Fergus had no choice but to wait patiently in case she should ever become free when her parents died, but her father lived to a grand old age and kept looking for another husband for her. It took him all of the next twenty years to find what he considered the right man for her, by which time she was in her forties. Fergus heard about her wedding and, having waited in vain, came back to see me at Lisdoonvarna only the other year, asking me to help him find a wife.

Now, they say that all is fair in love and war, but if you choose to mess with the true path of love it can have sad and serious effects.

Many years ago, when I was first matchmaking, a young

man and his aunt visited me. I was in the meadow saving hay. From a way off I could see a very old woman accompanied by a youngish man slowly walking across the valley and river to me. I was making lines of hay with a very young horse and a nine-foot wheelrake. This horse was a fabulous chestnut mare, almost like a racehorse. It was a pleasure working with her, she was so elegant. The woman arrived and explained that the man was her nephew, Gussy, and that he worked for the post office. Her voice was squeaky and seemed to scare the horse; it sounded like taking the lid off a rusty old tin can. She quickly squawked, 'Gussy needs a wife. He's going to give up his job as a postman and run the farm. We have five cows and the house was freshly slated just two years ago.' I asked her twice to stand away a little from the mare as it was her first day working with me and she was acting funny. I couldn't tell her that it was her voice that was frightening the horse.

My mother came down from the house, bringing out tea and scones, so we all sat down in the field by the cock of hay, discussing the match. There's no tea like tea in a meadow or bog. It must be the fresh air blending with the brew. The aunt turned to Gussy and said, 'If you meet a girl who can make tea like this, you'll be in heaven.'

We talked further and I suggested that Gussy should meet Maureen, a nice young girl for him, at Considine's pub in Ennistymon. He turned up with his friend Danny, who was a right character, a carefree, lovely young man, tall, handsome and full of fun. Maureen arrived shortly afterwards. She was delightful and sweet. The pub was lively, with good banter and fun. It was flying. There was a TV on, showing a music programme: Barney McKenna on banjo and Tony MacMahon on a button accordion were playing 'The Bucks of Oranmore', a great reel.

Danny jumped up and did a dance by himself on the great old flag floor. Halfway through Maureen hopped up and joined him. They danced and battered and battered the floor. Danny had hobnailed boots on, it was a spectacle. At the last few notes or bars of the tune, he lifted Maureen up in his arms and swung her round and around. I've danced all my life and seen a lot of dancing, but this was the best.

A sing-song started. Danny and Maureen could not take their eyes off each other; it was love at first sight. Gussy was quiet anyways, but had sensed what was going on and gotten quieter. Maureen came over and said to me, 'You got me a great match. He's lovely.' Theirs was a true love, which flourished and grew. Gussy, who had known she was intended for him, was very annoyed with me. I apologised and said I would find him another girl. He didn't seem interested, but things didn't rest there.

Danny and Maureen had a wonderful time together for about a year and a half. You'd always see them walking around holding hands, going to dances. Danny decided he would go to America to start a new life and planned to send Maureen her ticket after a while so she could join him. It was common enough that the fella would go out first, get set up a little bit, maybe find a job and a little place to stay, and write then for his girl to come.

One month, two months, three months passed and there was no word from Danny. He'd promised to write every week, and naturally enough she was heartbroken.

Gussy made it his business to meet up with Maureen, and as one year went by, then another, there was still no word from Danny. Everybody in town was saying, 'What kind of a man is he, to never contact her?' The truth, as you might have guessed, was that Gussy, the postman, had taken his best friend's letters as they arrived from America and hidden every single one of them. Gussy regularly proposed to Maureen who, in the absence of any news from Danny, eventually gave in and accepted his offer and they got married.

The story went that, many years later, Gussy died and Maureen decided to have their house renovated, taking all the thatch off. On knocking down an old wall in the house one of the tradesmen found seventy-three letters in a little bundle, all for Maureen. One of them had a ticket for her to join Danny in the States. Maureen never quite recovered from the shock and the grief that set in again.

A small drop of matchmaker's advice

♡ *When I think of the story of Gussy and Maureen, I recall the old adage, 'If you love someone, set them free. If they come back they're yours. If they don't they never were.' Even though it wasn't until Gussy was gone that Maureen found out what he'd done, I am fairly certain Gussy never lived a truly happy life, knowing his wife was meant to be with another, and Maureen most likely died with a broken heart. The truth will set you free. Deceit can imprison you for life.* ♡

Now the postman who delivered the mail to Ballingaddy would never have dreamt of such deviousness. He was straight as they came. He could never have hidden a stash of letters, because he was always awful curious to know what news, or more, they contained. My mother, who was a very hospitable kind, would invite him to come in for tea. And he'd want the letters to be opened before he'd leave. She might have the letter on the table and he wouldn't go until he'd said, 'Ah, that's from your sister Agnes,' or 'Is that from Elizabeth?' 'Is that from Dena, that letter?'

Well, she'd be happy to read out good news anyway, and he'd be happy enough to listen, that's the way it was. And if the letter was from America he'd be saying, 'I'd say there's dollars in that, Kathleen, I bet there's money in that.' An uncle of mine in the States used to send us a bit of money at Christmas, and sure enough the postman would be sitting across the kitchen table regular as clockwork, as he knew he would get his Christmas box at that time . . .

It was not only dollars that arrived from the States as a welcome surprise. Only the other year, one of the local lads, Paddy John Joe, asked me to find him a wife and wanted to discuss the possibilities with me. Whenever I suggested a place we could meet, he'd say, 'No, no, someone will see you with me and know you are helping me find a wife!' Eventually he suggested meeting me at an unused graveyard: just Paddy John Joe, his dog Spot, and me.

As we were discussing his chances of finding true love, two carloads of American visitors pulled up at the graveyard, searching for their ancestors called Murphy. Paddy John Joe shouted to me, 'Quick, Willie, get down, get down or they'll see us.' We weren't quite fast enough. The new arrivals caught sight of us and came across the graveyard towards us. Of course, we felt like two eejits lying there on the ground. I pretended to be scrabbling around looking for some keys; but when we stood up one of them recognised me as the matchmaker. My cover was blown.

I introduced Paddy John Joe as an eligible bachelor who had a small farm overlooking the sea. An American girl, about forty or so, was bending down patting and talking to Spot, when the little terrier jumped up and nipped her on the nose. Paddy ran over to comfort the woman, and jokingly I said, 'Well, you'll have to marry her now!' Everyone laughed, but her aunt, to my surprise, assisted me in encouraging them. The pair got married one year later, and now have two children and a happy life together. That's the way of things. Even when you try and control love, it can jump up and nip you on the nose when you least expect it.

Sometimes it takes a little longer to find the right mate, but patience pays off. That's what happened with Larry Dan.

There weren't many men around like Larry Dan. He was good-looking – tall, about six foot two – but he could carry it. He had a large farm and seemed happy enough being single. The years were rolling on and it didn't seem to bother him. He kept himself well; my father would say, 'Larry Dan is a bit like the "Mona Lisa" story: many dreams were brought to his doorstep, but they just lay there and died.' It was like a challenge and annoyance to people that he was escaping the married life and not tying the knot. Many remarks were passed, along the lines of 'The boat is passing Larry Dan by,' 'Oh, he'll be left on the shelf,' 'The woman hasn't been born yet that would please him.'

Larry Dan's mother was a teacher and he had been reared with a certain discipline that was obvious in his manner. On the surface he lacked a certain affection and ease. Larry was also an only son. An old drunken fellow said to me in a pub one time, 'An only son is a bad thing. I'll tell you, Willie Daly, my son is an only son and he is a bad thing. And I'm an only son myself, and I'm a bad thing too!'

But in truth it was hard to find fault with Larry Dan. He was manly and decent in a pub, enjoyed an occasional drink and would stand his round. He and I were good enough friends. And of course people were always saying to me, 'Willie, why don't you find Larry Dan a wife? It wouldn't affect his growth, now!' But Larry Dan never asked me.

There was a family called the Molloys who lived at the back of Slieve Elva mountain. The word 'respectable' went well with them. They were all quite good-looking. Three or four of the family went to England, where I heard they had good jobs. I liked this family: they were a bit wild but good fun. We would always have the craic and banter when they came into the pub in Ennistymon. One night we were getting ready to attend a social benefit dance at the Falls Hotel for a woman who had nineteen children and whose house had been partially destroyed by a fire. In the pub beforehand I was talking away with a clutch of the sisters from the family over in Slieve Elva, Mary, Susan and Alice. I was messing with them all, saying, 'Ah, you'll be like Biddy Kelly and have nineteen children each as well.'

'Feck off, Willie, didn't you ever hear of contraception?' they answered back.

'It's a sin to use it, though,' I said, solemnly like a priest, but joking.

Larry Dan was there too, now in his early forties. As in the past he was still an imposing figure of a man. I always felt a man was big prey for the girls between, say, twenty-four and thirty-six, and after that the sell-by date started creeping in. At forty-three, Larry Dan was still young, but was showing signs of all the toil needed to run his big farm and the years were clocking up. As we stood there a friend of Larry Dan's called Pat remarked how lovely the sisters looked, and Larry Dan commented how smart they were.

Larry Dan, Pat, the girls and I had many more drinks in the pub. We sang and danced and later all walked together down by the cascades, the famous waterfalls at Ennistymon, to Biddy Kelly's benefit dance at the Falls Hotel. Sections of the walk by the cascades were very muddy. The girls wanted to turn back so that their dance shoes wouldn't get destroyed, but the boys decided to be little Hercules and carried the girls up on their backs. Larry Dan whipped up Mary and brought her to dry ground. Pat took Susan. Larry Dan came back, bent down, and Alice jumped up on his back with her arms tightly around his neck. He jumped and bucked like a young colt. Alice laughed and screamed, hanging on for dear life, while her sisters pinched her and egged on Larry Dan to jump even more to try and throw her off. She hung on till we reached the door of the dance, where she gave Larry Dan a kiss and slipped to the ground.

The gaiety and frolics carried on at the dance, Alice and Larry Dan still buck-leaping around the floor. I'd never seen Larry Dan acting so youthful; he was like a young teenager out at his first dance. It was four o'clock by the time we left the Falls Hotel and still the happiness continued. Larry Dan was the happiest and drunkest of all, singing all the time, which was very much out of character.

A few days later Larry Dan came to my house, trying to recall the events of that night. He seemed bothered and distracted. He told me that the local priest, Father Tim, had called by his house to discuss dates and details for his wedding, and that the manager of the hotel had phoned up asking for a deposit for the reception. This was all news to Larry Dan. I couldn't help but laugh, and asked, 'Who is the lucky girl, then?' Scratching his head, Larry Dan smiled and said, 'Jesus, Willie, I don't know.' We both laughed, and he asked could I find out if it was Alice.

I poured him a couple of glasses of poteen. After a third glass he wondered out loud if he had proposed to Alice after they had gone for a walk down the glen by the river. We laughed more and more at the thought of the whole thing. With each glass of poteen he became more taken with the idea. We eventually finished the bottle and I suggested that there was nothing for it but to talk to Alice herself, and Larry Dan was happy with this.

As we drove up the bog road towards her family's house halfway up the mountain, I found myself wondering if this was really a good idea, but I said nothing and we kept on going. The girls had noticed the car coming and their mother was tying up the sheepdog as we drove into the yard. We were welcomed with great smiles by the girls, who were giggling and laughing. We had tea, sandwiches and apple cake. The girls took Larry Dan into the parlour for a good long time. Coming out smiling, he said, 'Willie, I'm getting married to Alice on the twentieth of June.' I shook his hand and congratulated them both.

The father of the family, who almost never said a word, took out another bottle of poteen and we drank and sang the night away. On my way home I thought to myself how wrong my assumptions about Larry Dan had been.

To find the spark of love, keep it alight and allow it to turn into an eternal flame, that is one of the matchmaker's arts. There is no formula to it, no secret recipe that works every time. If there was, believe me, I would distil it, because it would be a spirit with more of a knock-out blow than even the poteen with which we toasted the future happiness of Larry Dan and Alice.

9
The Trail of Love

One Garland Sunday when I was maybe seven or eight, a group of summer visitors stopped by Ballingaddy to meet my father. They arrived in a flotilla of horse-drawn carts. I stepped out to admire their carts and the horses waiting outside in the lane, and I can vividly remember thinking to myself, as I stood looking at these lovely horses, One day when I get older, I will get myself eight of these fine horses.

Garland Sunday was the last Sunday of July, a great annual holiday anticipating the coming harvest season. From ten in the morning I could hear the sound of the horses and carts passing Kellys Cross on the way to the coast, coming down from Kilfenora and Corofin. Few of the jaunting cars had rubber tyres, just iron bands around the wooden wheels. The wheels sounded like music, accompanying the clattering of

the horses' hooves, the chattering of the families, the squeal-
ing of the kids overexcited at the prospect of a day by the sea,
their legs kicking in joy as they dangled over the edge of the
jaunting car. It was a real carnival atmosphere.

We were lucky: we lived close to the sea and could see
the shore from our front door. But most people inland
would only get a chance to go to the sea occasionally. We
used to join them later on for the celebrations over at
Lahinch, where the whole street was covered with travelling
amusements and all the pubs were roaring. In the evening
we usually got back home earlier than most families, since
my parents were never big drinkers. Now we would hear all
the carts rolling back and this time a more raucous shouting and carrying on, and if they were trotting any bit at all
through the fading light we could see the sparks flying up
off the road, from the iron and the hooves on flint and
stone. There was nothing quite like driving through the
countryside in a trap or jaunting car, your way lit only by
candlelight, the bushes and trees suddenly caught in the
glow, and beyond, ahead and behind nothing but pure
pitch black.

One of my very earliest memories is of going in our jaunting car to Kilfenora, to watch the horse races there with the
man from over the road, Fahey, a very good horseman. My
father was never very comfortable with horses. We owned
some, of course, as there was a lot of ploughing to be done,
harrowing and opening drills, you had to, but he wouldn't be

too skilled with the horses, whereas I always enjoyed working with them. I've been at them all my life.

I have always had a natural empathy with horses, and maybe it's a similar sense that I have been able to use when it comes to matchmaking. It's true that if you can understand horses you are usually good at understanding those strange and unpredictable creatures called people. A journalist once called me 'the horse whisperer of romance', a description which I took with a hefty serving of salt, but none the less I accepted it as a compliment.

Around the time that I opened my first matchmaking office, in the Irish Arms in Lisdoonvarna, I started running pony treks and riding holidays around the area. Our first ever advert is still on the wall of the Roadside Tavern in Lisdoonvarna. At the start of the pony-trekking I hadn't seen it as complementary to my matchmaking. I was living out the dream I had at seven of owning eight horses just like those I had seen on that Garland Sunday. As I set about it, very good friends of mine said, 'Would you start with two horses and see how it goes?'

'No, two would be no good, it must be eight,' and I made sure that I had exactly eight fine horses, no more, no less, on the first day that we opened for business. Horses were very plentiful at that time: a lot of people still didn't have tractors then so I was able to borrow the extra horses and ponies I needed.

I ran a number of different trails, but the best by far was the

Love Trail: six days travelling gently along wonderfully scenic routes, breathtaking views from the Carrig Mountains, over the hills to Galway, Connemara and the bay, all with a view to finding love.

The Love Trail was the idea of my daughter Marie. She wanted to take advantage of our beautiful natural surroundings. Marie described the trail as 'a hidden treasure for everyone to find. It is hidden in oneself and is ignited by those enchanted surroundings, beautiful horses and pleasure-filled evenings.' The Love Trail took off like a racehorse, especially once a BBC television crew came with us and made a documentary about it, that was a big boost.

In each of the groups there would be a mixture of people who were quite seriously looking for love along with a few who were taking the holiday in a more light-hearted way. Now horses are canny, and can be very good judges of humans. If they decide it's a good idea, they might just allow two of the riders to move a little closer as they ride along, and then keep them alongside each other as their conversation grows and a relationship develops. I guess that's why they call it horse sense.

At the start of a Love Trail we would meet everyone at Shannon Airport and take them to their accommodation and on to an introductory evening at our family pub, Daly's in the main street of Ennistymon, an old authentic pub with what were called 'the best Irish evenings in the world' – mind you, that was by people who were drunk. There would be music on the fiddles, harps and banjos, flutes and *bodhráns*, and Jamesie Keating playing the spoons and singing, and of course great dancing.

The resident musicians were the Killoughery brothers, Paddy and John, Paddy wearing an old cap and playing fiddle and John, the flute player, wearing a small hat. They were both of a decent age and fitted so well into the old bar. There they were joined by John Leary, an accordion player, and Tom Driscoll on the concertina. Another great flute player was Tony O'Leary, known as 'Timber Tony' because not only did he play a wooden flute but he had a wooden leg. Other regulars were Tony O'Loughlan, Sean Murphy and Eileen O'Donoghue, all great accordion players, Johnny Beggan, a Dubliner who played the banjo and sang ballads, and Blind Steven, a great singer and guitarist who somehow was the one to see everybody home safely. It was a mystery how he did this.

Many visitors from Dublin came to the pub: Debby Burke would sing 'When the Lights Go Out in Old Dublin Town'; Teresa Organ always brought the house down with 'Among the Fields of Barley'; and a great friend of mine, Johnny Mahony, would recite poems both in English and in Irish. Johnny added a great flavour to a good evening. The music would start good, but be indescribable by the end of the evening: the expression that the music would 'lift the roof of the house' was spot on. I often felt that the magic of the music had intoxicated the minds, the bodies and souls of the guests.

A small drop of matchmaker's advice

♡ I am a great believer in the power of music. Music leads to dancing, and dancing to romance. As my mother often said, 'Sometimes the song is short but the chorus is long.' The Irish used to dance before going into battle, and it also helps prepare the soul for love. The jigs and reels are invigorating: they get the heart pumping and the blood moving. And whenever I am playing music in one of the pubs in Ennistymon or Doolin, with singers, accordionists or fiddle players, the magic is in the listening to each other, and giving space for everyone to play. In any relationship we can all listen harder, not just to what our partner is saying, but – and often more importantly – to what they haven't *said out loud. ♡*

After a night in the bar, we would set out on the trail. It was always great to observe the initial stages of eagerness and the anticipation of falling in love. The hope and thought of love are wonderful. We would encourage the riders to throw caution away. American visitors would quickly do so, but some of our other guests needed a little bit more time to release their emotions. A pint of Guinness never failed to help. Although I would never encourage anyone to marry a drunkard, it is always useful to see a prospective partner – if they're not teetotal – with a drink or few inside them. The seemingly perfect partner can be deceptive. There may be no obvious sign of wildness or unpredictability but if it is lying dormant it is best to see it come to the fore early on rather than taking you by surprise.

There was a time on the treks when one of the riders shedding her inhibitions certainly took some of the local men by surprise. Maybe ten years ago we were up at Lake Lickeen one evening after taking the horses for a ride on a baking-hot summer's day. This lovely girl from Holland who had been riding with us came too, and asked if it was all right for her to go swimming. 'Sure,' I said. 'Help yourself.' So she took all her togs off in front of us and jumped naked into the water. Now, there was a rake of fellows saving hay in the meadow next to the lake and I couldn't resist saying to them, 'Lads, can you come and give me a hand to hold these horses?' And I must say they were awful keen to help.

This girl didn't mind. She emerged from the water, cool as you like, totally refreshed from her dip in the lake, strolled out among the midst of them, towelled herself down, got dressed and swung herself back on her horse. She didn't see anything wrong – why should she? She was just going out for a swim. I looked around. There were a lot of open mouths amongst the lads holding the horses. Jesus, they were just gaping. I don't think they had ever seen a naked woman up close before, even though some of them were married. For a month and more after, I swear, those guys were up at the lake every day, whenever they saw the horses, praying for a repeat performance.

During the Love Trail we would pick the horses from our stable to suit the riders as carefully as I would select romantic partners, and as we wound through the Clare countryside, I would sometimes suggest a change of horse for the following day if I could see some potential for love between the riders. This was because certain horses got on well with each other and if, for instance, Mary was riding Brad Pitt (I call all the horses after film stars) and seemed to be responding romantically to Kevin, but he was on a horse that Brad Pitt was not so comfortable with, I would swap Kevin on to Pamela Anderson, a horse Brad Pitt enjoyed trekking alongside, so that the riders could stay close throughout the day.

Up to twenty people would ride the Love Trail at one time, starting off on the first day up to Lickeen Lake across the other side of Kellys Cross, and then back along the Green River Road, a gentle easy ride, mainly walking and trotting, of three and a half hours. This was a loosener, a chance for everybody to settle even further into a relaxed mood. I was happy with this, as I would be surprised to detect any emotion between the riders on this first day.

Day two was a beach ride, about four hours' duration, with a fair amount of time spent at the beach, at O'Looney's surf pub in Lahinch. Our first Love Trail marriage started here, between Jennifer, a girl from California, and Michael, a local fisherman in his late twenties. Michael was a good fisherman, but not at all happy on a horse. Jennifer willingly helped him feel comfortable. Her kindness and gentleness overcame his lack of confidence, and by the following spring they were married, and now have three children.

Our trail guide in the beginning was our cousin Sean Kelly. He had lived with our family for a while as a young lad, and left for Dublin at the age of thirteen. When he returned to the area he was an ideal addition to our team. Apart from being a good rider he could entertain the guests: he was good-looking, with big blue eyes and blond hair, always funny, a great storyteller, all the guests loved him. Sean also met his partner on the Love Trail, though now, God bless him, he has passed away. And the girls who helped on the rides also felt the romance: two lovely girls, one from Germany, the other from America, both fell in love with local fellas and married them.

By day three the group would be ready to tackle the Cliffs of Moher ride, a great six-hour hack through the fabulous countryside, stopping off at St Bridget's Well outside Liscannor, dropping into Considine's or Murphy's pub nearby, sitting on the wall outside and watching the boats move in and out of Liscannor Bay. As this was the third day of the trail people had begun loosening up and emotions were intensifying. My daughter Marie and son Rory were always good at detecting who was interested in who. And at this stage even the horses seemed to know and hang out together.

The fourth day was one of my favourites, up into the Carrig and Bahourough mountain trail, a stunning ride through bogs and mountains. I spent much of my younger life cutting turf for the winter's fire on those mountains and know every inch of them.

On the fifth day of the trail we left Doolin and headed up into the Burren, three and a half hours along the green roads of the lunar-like landscape and its spectacular array of wild flowers with views over Galway Bay, Connemara and the Aran Islands, and passing by castles and ruined monasteries before heading to O'Donoghue's pub in Fanore. A lovely surprise awaited our guests here, as for a century or more the pub has hosted afternoon dancing. Things got a little competitive here as the men riding on the trail had to compete with the local men on the dance floor for the girls. Even the thought of one of the Fanore boys moving in on a particular girl often encouraged a visitor to make his first move.

One year not so long ago we had three proposals of marriage on this fifth day. One from a Dublin boy to a girl from the Netherlands, an English boy to an Irish girl from Limerick, and a Clare boy to an American woman, all of them in their mid-twenties to early thirties. I always feel it is difficult for a man not to propose, and almost impossible for a woman to say no, in these wonderful surroundings. It would be easy with the romantic environment, deep among the lanes lined with the hawthorn and the hedgerows, striding over the limestone outcrops of the Burren or letting the Atlantic winds freshen your mind as you watch the sunset from the top of the cliffs.

The following day we'd ride even deeper into the Burren.

It was heaven. And now or never for most of the Love Trail bunch. I always noticed the extra attention given to the girls. Marie would suggest that the men make use of the natural surroundings, and all the vibrant flowers. The girls felt a little spoilt, as the flowers would make the answer to the proposal easy. Our final lunch stop was the Kilshanny pub, which used to be the home of one of my old schoolteachers, Mrs Considine.

A high number of people found true love through riding with the horses. I must say I feel the surroundings of the Burren played a big part. Its magnificence makes man feel insignificant.

There was one day when I had an inkling that two romances might bloom, during a four-and-a-half-hour trail across the Burren. There was a couple who I could see were already getting fond of each other on the previous days, but I also noticed a fella starting to spend a lot of time with an American girl from down near Memphis who had had very little experience of riding before. She had surprised me by how quickly she had got used to the long days of riding. There were people whose arses would get awful sore after four or five days, but she seemed totally content and comfortable. Your man was there dancing attention to her, she probably knew that. He was a local enough lad, who had only joined the trail for a couple of days in the hope of meeting somebody, and it had clicked. She was probably about thirty-five, a very fine girl, happy and full of good fun.

On the way back a huge storm blew up out of nowhere, gales and gusts of ninety miles an hour turned out. I went back to the farm with one of my sons to fetch a couple of cars and trailers. By the time we got back to the group, even the most experienced riders had decided they'd get off, they'd had quite enough. This wind was blasting, the rain lashing, branches of trees blowing off and flying about, an awful experience you could say, but also terribly exciting. It certainly heightened the emotions. On that particular day the two couples I'd had in mind started a relationship and both of them went on to get married.

A small drop of matchmaker's advice

♡ *Love is often like a wild horse, unpredictable and headstrong. But if you stay calm, you can rein in even the most difficult colt. From the very first match I ever made, I understood that half the battle is creating a natural situation for a couple to meet. That was why the Love Trail was a perfect place for romance to evolve. Perhaps more importantly, I have learnt that the situation can be something very ordinary, very mundane, with no undue pressure. By being able to talk about something that has nothing to do with personal feelings, it's frequently at that point that the first, vital little crackle of electricity passes between two people.* ♡

Now just in case you think that horses will always help engineer a happy ending, I'd better tell you the tale of Moira Rua O'Brien. She was part of the great O'Brien family, who owned many of the castles in this region four or five hundred years ago. Moira was an extremely attractive woman, maybe five foot ten with a beautiful head of flaming-red hair falling down way past her waist; that was the meaning of her name, Moira Rua, 'red-haired Mary'.

Fadó, fadó, as we say – a long, long time ago, Moira owned one of the biggest castles in the area, certainly the largest that I know of around here, as it still stands there in the centre of the Burren. It's called Leamanagh Castle, but I have always known it as Moira Rua's Castle. There she had her own garrison of soldiers, perhaps as many as eleven hundred men, so if she wanted to find a suitor she could take her pick from one of these fellows and marry them. But she had such a choice of men, and she was such a passionate woman, that after two or three months she would get bored with the husband and want a new one.

Usually she would brutally dispatch the old husband by bayoneting him on the top of the castle tower and pitching him over the edge. But on a few occasions, if she found she liked the husband, she would offer him the prospect of a reprieve for an extra three months. It was not a lot, but better than dying, and at least there was a gleam of hope. Moira Rua kept an evil black stallion in the dungeon of the castle. So she would say that if the husband could master her black horse that would be the key to a second term with her.

But the minute the rider got himself up in the saddle, the black stallion would gallop away out of control and head for the Cliffs of Moher, which were ten miles away, with a posse of Moira's henchmen riding in pursuit. As soon as the horse reached the cliffs, bang, he'd stick his hooves in the ground and the rider would be flung down over the edge to his death. So it really wasn't much of a deal she was offering.

One day, after she had seen off seventeen husbands, she chose one particular boy to be her next groom, a cousin of hers, one Donnach Dubh O'Brien, 'Black Dennis', a powerful young man with jet-black hair. I suppose he fell in love with her as she was a beautiful-looking woman, but equally he knew what she was capable of and what his fate might be. As the end of his first three months with Moira approached he went to see his father and told him that his time was nearly up but that he had the choice of riding her black stallion.

His father said, 'Ask her if you can use your own bridle.' So Donnach went back to the castle and Moira agreed to him using it. Donnach chose one that was as strong and unbreakable as he could find. Come the day and up he got on the stallion, and as usual the horse pelted as hard as it could straight for the cliffs. The young lad was pulling and pulling on the bridle.

Donnach was exceptionally strong and eventually, a short

distance from the cliffs, he pulled so hard that he broke the horse's neck.

When Moira heard the news that he had succeeded in defeating her horse, she was totally infuriated. She went out into the stables, saddled up her own horse and started lashing him around the area of the castle. As she was riding and riding, spitting with fury, with all that red hair blowing in the wind with the movement of the horse, her hair got caught in the limb of a tree and she was hanged by the hair of her own head.

I always wondered whether she had been driven to that fury by missing her black stallion more than Donnach Dubh, or whether Donnach had won his way into her heart.

Working with the horses provided one unexpected bonus, when I found myself working on a film set for three months with Richard Burton. This was in the spring of 1980. A crew came over to Clare to make a film called *Lovespell*, the tale of Tristan and Isolde. Richard Burton was Mark, the King of Cornwall, and the actress playing Isolde was Kate Mulgrew, who had starred on TV in *Mrs Columbo*. The story was that King Mark came to Ireland, met this girl Isolde, the daughter of an Irish king, fell in love with her and couldn't get her out of his mind. He went back to England, but this girl stayed in his mind. He sent his nephew Tristan over to deliver a marriage proposal and bring her back – they must have been very simple times then: 'Go over and bring that lady back for me.' Tristan was handsome; she was young and attractive. On the way back to Cornwall they fell in love and all hell broke loose.

The film company came in looking for horses. I had a dozen or so that I could give them, and they needed more from elsewhere, of course, because they had an army of soldiers chasing Tristan and Isolde. There was a nice bit of money for every horse and each had to have a rider so I roped in the young lads who worked for me. I was happy that everyone was making a few shillings out of it as well.

The first scene I was involved in was up in Doolin along the beach, with maybe thirty horses. Everything was set up, the lorries and trailers, the whole scenario. There was a man overseeing the horses. Now neither Kate Mulgrew nor Richard Burton could ride very well. They had a beautiful, exotic, pure-cream horse for her, and he had a huge black Irish horse, fabulous, awful calm. Her horse wasn't so quiet, though. John, the guy in charge of the horses, said, 'We'll keep them moving around.' I wondered out loud if that was such a good idea, since the horses were not used to each other; perhaps we should leave them until they were needed. But he probably wanted to impress the crowd. So grand, he was the boss. 'We'll ride to the point over there,' he said.

The next thing, didn't his horse put her leg into a rabbit's burrow or a fox hole? She came up like a shot, knocked him off and he broke his shoulder. He was lying on the ground in a great deal of pain. Richard Burton came over in his costume, long robes flying behind him. That was my first time meeting him. He asked, 'What's wrong with this man?'

'Ach,' I said, 'he's suffering from an old hangover there from last night.' I couldn't resist it. The crew thought it was a great answer to give him, because he was so apprehensive about riding that he didn't want to hear about anyone falling.

The whole thing had to be cancelled that day. I think Kate Mulgrew had got too nervous. They rang me during the day and said, 'John is going to be recuperating for a while. Would you be interested in helping out?' The following day they wanted thirty horses out again. I went down to the dole office and offered the job to the fellas that I knew would be able to get up on the horses.

Everything went off grand, and later they were looking for stand-ins for the stars. 'Would you do it for Richard Burton, Willie?'

'I would now.' I don't think I had a notion what being a stand-in meant. So I ended up working with the film for three months

On the final night of filming, everybody headed for one of the local pubs. Two of the regular musicians, Paddy and John Kelly, were asked to play. Paddy replied in his low musical voice, 'We can't. We are very tired as we were playing all weekend in Doolin.'

The man organising the music said, 'But, Paddy, it's for Richard Burton.'

Paddy thought for a moment and replied, 'Well, we don't

know him, but maybe he knows us. We'll play.' Paddy and John had never heard of Richard Burton. Later on that evening Richard joined in the music with his spoons. It was a grand night.

Back on the Love Trail, we regularly used to pass one house on the Carrig and Bahourough Mountains. It belonged to a widow woman who had lots of children. She had a great saying with a few drinks in her: 'I have a large family, but my husband was small, God rest his soul.' Four of her sons were still with her on the farm. Whenever we passed the house with the horses she would come out and ask, 'Willie, have you any nice girls for my sons Michael, John, Neddy and Kevin?'

I knew it would be easy to match them, as they were tall, dark and handsome. Each time we went past the mother would come out with drinks or bottles of tea to share with the guests. And always she gave a couple of eggs to the female riders. She would wrap them in paper and with a laugh put them in the girls' pockets. Her sons would either be out in the bogs or the garden near the house. She would start shouting, 'Come out, Michael, John, come out, come here and meet these lovely girls who ride out with Willie.'

Michael and John, both in their late twenties, were shy, though not unfriendly. Living up the mountain they would not meet many people. In the first year of the trail I introduced them to Eleanor and Cindy, two English girls. They hit it off well, and it was easy to make their match. Both couples got married shortly afterwards. By the third year Mary had also succeeded in getting her last two sons married. Now when I pass her house she salutes me through the kitchen window, though I sometimes feel she might regret having been so successful in making those matches, as she now lives alone and must miss her boys a lot.

I recently met her in a shop in Ennistymon and partly in jest she asked me, 'Willie, would you have any old fellow who would suit me?'

I replied, 'Mary, you know the saying: "There's no old shoe but there is a stocking to fit."'

She laughed more and went on her way. I am quietly looking for somebody for her, a man who could live up a mountain and be happy with Mary.

10
Riding the Tiger

Sport plays a massive part in people's lives in Ireland. Some would live and die and talk about nothing else but their teams. Debates become heated and fights even break out. Hurling is huge in Clare and the excitement, tension and even sense of fear before a big match are unbelievable.

In 1995 the Clare hurling team made it to the All-Ireland final, which would be played on Sunday 3 September at GAA headquarters – Croke Park, Dublin – during the Match-making Festival.

Lisdoonvarna was a sea of saffron and blue, the county colours, with flags flying from anything that could hold one up, bunting stretching from one side of the street to the other, all the shop and pub windows decorated. Even some rival flags for our opponents, Offaly, were on display.

Tickets to the match were like gold dust. That year the

first question everyone asked, rather than 'Willie, can you get me a wife?', was 'Willie, any chance of getting me a ticket?' Fellas were wandering around with signs pinned to their shirts: TICKET WANTED. Anyone with any access to tickets would have to leave their phone off the hook as it would ring so often, always with the same request. People were desperate.

The Friday evening before the match, you could cut the excitement with a knife in Lisdoonvarna. Everyone was going to town on the exuberance of it all that evening, as there would be a mass exodus on the Saturday, with a huge contingent heading off to see the match in Dublin, all shouting, 'C'mon the Banner,' beating *bodhráns* as though they were war drums and chanting, 'Come out, Biddy Early, and we'll beat the curse out of you, and then we'll beat the stuffing out of Offaly.' Biddy Early was a local woman known as a witch who had reportedly put a curse on Clare hurling, saying they would not win an All-Ireland title for eighty years. It was now eighty-one years since Clare had last won a title.

I was sitting in my office in the Matchmaker pub – it was full to busting – and listening to yet another prediction of how the match would go. Mattie was in his early fifties and had come into town with seven or eight young men from his own club. He was a stalwart hurling-club member, who had devoted his whole life to the sport and never missed a match. He had even bought an old Ford Transit van to bring the lads, with all their gear, the boots and hurley sticks, to matches, which the lads had painted blue and yellow. They loved Mattie and Mattie loved them. He had taken care of them for so long and now they were minding him and wanted to give him the time of his life.

The lads all had tickets for the match and didn't need to ask me if I knew how to find some, so their first question when they came into my office was 'Willie, could you find a woman for Mattie?' Each of them would suggest a quality she would have to have: she'd have to love hurling, be a good cook, 'Love all of us,' one said, 'Keep Mattie warm in bed,' 'Big tits!' another interrupted. Mattie laughed and said he wouldn't object to any of those.

As we were laughing with Mattie, three or four girls, quite well cut and all wearing Clare jerseys, half fell into the office. One asked me, 'Where's the form? I want a man who's tall, dark, handsome, lots of money, a cottage with a good view of the sea and his own teeth!' Another devil with tumbling red hair added, 'And well hung, Willie, he has to be well hung!'

Everyone was roaring and laughing at this and then Geraldine, another redhead with a face full of freckles, shouted, 'I'll marry the first man to give me a ticket for the match.'

One of her friends yelled back, 'You'll have more chance of bedding the Clare captain tonight!'

With that Mattie reached into the pocket of his shirt,

pulled out his piece of gold – his ticket to the match – and stretched over to offer it to her.

You could hear a pin drop. For a moment the world stopped. All eyes were on Geraldine. Her face changed and for a minute I thought she was going to say no. The seconds seemed like hours – then a big smile crossed her face. She rushed over to Mattie and threw her arms around him while everyone cheered and clapped. The party raged into the early hours. I have rarely seen such happiness and joy: it was like the hen night, stag night, wedding day and honeymoon all rolled into one. Not only did Geraldine keep to her promise – she and Mattie were married the next spring – but Clare won the match (for the hurling fans amongst you, the final score was 1–13 to 2–8). It was a match made over a match. Could life be any better?

Life was generally good in Ireland in the 1980s and 90s. We've all heard of the Celtic Tiger. After decades – centuries – of make do and mend for most people, there were new money and prospects. No wonder everyone wanted to jump up on the tiger's back.

There was certainly a noticeable change at the Lisdoonvarna festival. What rekindled it a good deal was the starting up of a Barbecue Championship and the Lisdoonvarna Music Festival, which created great excitement even though it only ran for six years. Christy Moore wrote a wonderful song called 'Lisdoonvarna' that summed up the fun we had there.

The Music Festival was held just outside the town during July for the first few years, but the ground in that field was awful wet, and they shifted the whole event closer to Doolin for the last three years. Although the music didn't impinge so much on the matchmaking, I have great memories of that festival. Most years they'd say, 'Can you come over, Willie, and talk about the matchmaking?' so I'd be interviewed up on the stage between acts. It was out of season, of course, but it was a grand advert for the matchmaking none the less.

There was a raft of changes throughout Ireland in those years of the 1980s and 90s. You could notice it most with all the building work that went on, brand-new houses sprouting up everywhere. I was one who loved the old style of thatched cottages, but it seemed as if no one wanted that look any more. It was as if the whole nation wanted to move on, to forget the hardships and struggles of the past, to leave those times behind; anything that harked back to the old rural way of life was out of favour.

West Clare was no exception. Over in Doolin you couldn't move for dump-trucks and scaffolding lorries. The old individual family-run shops on the main street in Ennistymon suddenly had to compete with an enormous superstore that went up right where Larry's Lane had been. At the Cliffs of Moher the tourist board built a visitor centre dug deep into the hillside that looked like something straight out of a James Bond movie.

A new generation of entrepreneurs arrived in Lisdoon-varna and took over some of the hotels, including the old Hydro. It was time for a change, and I have to admit they injected a fresh energy. And they brought in a younger crowd. I was in the Hydro one day when Jim White, the new owner of the place, introduced me to many people, saying, 'This is Willie Daly, the matchmaker.'

Jim brought a new energy and life to Lisdoonvarna; there was no finishing time for Jim. If the craic was good, Jim would keep the Hydro open all night. The White family were one of the big players, and they still do put an awful lot of work into it, with half a dozen hotels, including White's and the new Burren Castle Hotel out near Doolin. These changes unsettled a few people locally, but gave the Matchmaking Festival a mighty rejuvenation, by promoting it much more widely and organising new events and attractions.

There was maybe a certain percentage of people in the town who weren't in favour of the extra push the festival was getting, perhaps concerned about bringing in a different crowd, younger, maybe rowdier, more interested in drinking than dancing. I always tried to keep out of any politics. I just go along and I do what I do, but I was always sure that even those who were not great fans were happy enough to get the new crowds in and the money they brought with them.

One of the shifts – and the one that affected me most directly – was a much higher number of visitors arriving from overseas. There had always been a few who would hear about the festival during a late-summer trip to Ireland and go out of their way to travel over to County Clare and swing by. But now we found a new influx of visitors – particularly from America – flying in specifically for the festival.

This influx reopened my eyes to the appeal of the Matchmaking Festival – I had been going for so long, man and boy, that it seemed a natural part of the fabric of my life. I remember one woman from New York, who had a healthy dose of Irish blood in her veins, telling me over a pint of Guinness at the Roadside Tavern about her first memories of the festival. 'I walked into the Spa Wells,' she said, 'and it was as if I was stepping out of a time machine. The dances, the music, these pubs which feel like they have been around for ever. There is nothing like this back home.' She paused to take another sip and wave to a new friend over at the bar. 'And the best thing is, you don't just get to watch it like a tourist, you experience it.'

'I know what you mean,' I agreed. 'You'll have barely sat down before some charming Irish fella is asking you to dance, and probably proposing marriage before the evening is much older – and throwing ten cows and twenty acres of land into the bargain!'

In particular there were suddenly a lot of older American women in town. They came over from a completely different kind of environment, and an opulent enough past, but when they arrived in Lisdoonvarna I remarked a strange phenomenon. It was not usually the most glamorous fellas they were looking for. This often surprised me. Here were these women, certainly in their late forties or fifties and often in their sixties and seventies, getting an awful lot of attention, loads of fellas – and I'm talking about lads as young as twenty-four going after a woman who was maybe forty years older.

All of a sudden a woman spending time at the festival would pick somebody who was the total opposite to what she was familiar with. Now, she might have come out of at least two, maybe three marriages, and would be probably well off enough, but the one thing she didn't have was love. So over she comes to Ireland and meets some old fella who's half drunk, getting up off the floor, dancing a little, singing an old song, and she would get intrigued by him, they would kind of click. He might be a rough-looking character, bad teeth, hair uncombed, his clothes not done too well, but she could envisage another person there.

The man can't believe that this lovely woman would be attracted to him. She has recognised something in him which the Irish girls don't. The local girls take one look, say, 'Ah, that drunken old fellow,' and pass him out. But this American divorcée or widow can see the makings of great material. It's like buying an old farmhouse that's been neglected for a number of years and needs some repairs: she can picture what she might be able to achieve with a little restyling and a fair old makeover.

In three years' time we'd see him coming back smelling like roses, some extra weight around his middle, his hair cut neat, his clothes smartened and his teeth done up as well. And after another three or four years she loses interest and has to go off looking for another fella to do up – well, maybe I'm exaggerating there. But, with all the alterations and his new respectable looks, his own attitude will probably have changed too. And that can be a mistake. This woman liked the person she met in Ireland, then tried to mould him to the way she'd like him to be, and not necessarily what he wanted. And, Jesus, sometimes I'd say, 'He was such a great character, it's a pity he has changed with all these good clothes and new manners.'

When I was younger, a lot of my friends went down this route, especially the musicians, who were just having a marvellous time, because women fancied them. I saw a good number of them coming back to Ireland after fifteen years in a new life, and they wouldn't seem to be alive at all. Everything would be in a controlled fashion, and to me that would seem as if they were nearly dead. They'd have to check with the wife if they could do this or do that or could they go out for the night to the pub, instead of just walking out. But if the couple decides to stay in Ireland the man won't change, that is the funny thing. The new wife actually becomes more Irish!

There was a real level of culture shock on both sides. I remember one group of a dozen women coming to Lisdoonvarna from America to find partners. This was during the mid-1980s. They were being accompanied by a journalist who was writing a piece for a paper, and she asked me to go up with them of an evening. I met this writer at about half-past seven and we were chatting away. She said, 'Now, Willie, the group are quite disappointed that they haven't met anyone yet.'

'Well, I'm here every night,' I said. 'Where are they?'

'They've eaten and gone to bed,' she replied.

I laughed. 'Do you realise,' I said, 'that any Irish man doesn't have even a notion of an emotion until after twelve o'clock at night, and he has twenty pints of Guinness drank?'

This corner of Ireland was introduced to many people thanks to the TV show *Father Ted*. If you've never seen it, find yourself a DVD. Watching the antics of Fathers Ted, Dougal and Jack on Craggy Island is a great way of understanding the quirky ways of life in rural Ireland and the Irish sense of humour. And in an episode or two you might see a certain bearded matchmaker moving through the crowds.

Most of the outdoor locations for the show were shot in and around the area. The actors and the crew stayed in the Falls Hotel in Ennistymon, so after a day's filming they would wander up into the town and head for Cooley's, or Eugene's or our bar, Daly's. They were a friendly crowd and many of them still pop by if they are in the area. Ted, Jack and Dougal – I always think of them by their characters' names – would come in a good lot, on and off, and we got to know them.

Father Jack loved to play the fiddle, and this was a time when we had plenty of traditional music in the bar. Jack never played with the main men, but he would get up and play a solo; he was very good on the airs like 'The Cuilan' or 'The Lonesome Boatman' and he also played some jigs and reels: 'The Irish Washerwoman' and 'The Geese in the Bog' were his favourites. He'd wait his turn like everybody else, and people would be appreciative of it.

From time to time the crew might pop into the pub and say to Marie, who was usually working behind the bar, or to one of my daughters, 'Can you gather together three or four fellas and a couple of girls, for tomorrow? We need some extras.' Everyone was excited, of course. As the show came on the TV it was lovely to recognise so many faces – Ignatius Commane, Mona Davies, Micky McCormac – and my own daughters Marie, Elsha and Sarah were in the 'Lovely Girls' competition that Father Ted judged.

The scene was shot in Kilfenora and there was a bunch of us over there for the day, with Paddy Daly, a cousin of mine. Now Paddy really liked his drink when he'd be out, a very bright man, interested in politics, a great memory for retaining information and a powerful amount of conversation. He was a very good farmer, but it wasn't really his thing. His parents left him the farm and that is what he'd had to do.

We spent the morning walking about this marquee, carrying pints of fake beer, laughing and joking. At the lunch break Paddy and a few more, six of us, all locals, decided we would go down to Vaughan's in Kilfenora, and I had a whiskey myself, and Paddy had one, then someone else got a drink in. The big surprise to me was that my cousin Paddy, and he was not known to hurry out of a pub, all of a sudden said, very seriously, 'Willie, look at the time it is, we're needed back on the set. We'll have to go back.' I couldn't believe it, but he was so excited about his part in the performance that he was quite happy, eager even, to stop drinking. That stayed in my mind: 'Come on, come on, lads, we have to go back.'

At the wrap night party for one of the series, I got talking to Frank Kelly, who played Father Jack. He said, 'Willie, is there anywhere I can get some poteen? I have some actor friends coming from London and I want it as a special surprise for them.' I said, 'Frank, I know a ninety-year-old woman who has some real good stuff for sale. Her husband died a few years ago and she gave me a few bottles for safekeeping.' 'Great,' he said. 'Get me two bottles.'

I got the bottles and gave them to Frank the following day. Both bottles were marked 'Holy Water'. It's said that this practice was started by nuns bringing back the illegal poteen from Ireland to their various nunneries. It was the only way to get it through customs. In one instance the customs man checked the bottles and informed the two nuns that this was not Holy Water but alcohol. Both nuns blessed themselves hurriedly repeating that 'the power of the Lord is unlimited' – and made it through customs.

Another story goes that in Mother Theresa's final days she was failing fast and refusing to eat or drink except for a little milk. A little Irish nun who had just returned from Ireland put some poteen into Mother Theresa's milk and a glow came into her cheeks. There was always a big congregation of priests and nuns in Mother Theresa's chamber, continuously asking her whether there were any secrets from heaven she wanted to reveal before she passed away. As she seemed to revive one of the priests said again, 'Are there any words of wisdom you want to leave us with?' Mother Theresa shot up in the bed and said, 'Don't sell that cow.'

So Frank Kelly's guests turned up and he produced his two bottles of poteen. He poured them a glass each and waited for a reaction. One of the guests smelt it, tasted it gingerly and swallowed the glassful before saying, 'Frank, this is water!' I later realised that a young man fond of the drink and knowing where I kept the poteen hidden had drunk all the poteen and filled the bottles with water . . .

A small drop of matchmaker's advice

♡ *The Celtic Tiger was a good lesson for matchmaking as well. There was great opportunity in Ireland during these years, and many lives were changed for ever. Some took the opportunity to work hard and make good choices for their business and family, while other people got greedy and took short-term gambles that didn't pay off in the end. This is much like the Lisdoonvarna festival itself and the people who attend that are armed with ten pints of Guinness. So many people come and see all the choices for a match and they can't make up their minds who they want to talk to. It's exactly like a child in a sweet shop. When they may be having great craic with one person, they'll see someone more handsome across the room and bam, just like that they have to have him. I try to make people focus a bit more. Commit to having a nice long conversation and a dance or two. When an opportunity presents itself you have to grab it and give it all you've got. Pursuing too many choices lessens your chances of success.* ♡

A number of years back an American woman came into the Matchmaker Bar, in her late thirties, very attractive, tall, good-looking, dressed in black. She talked to me for a minute along with one or two of her friends, who I already knew. A particular gentleman rushed over to me who had been watching this: 'Willie, Willie, would you introduce me to that woman?' No problem. I went over and introduced them, and almost the first thing he said to her was 'God, you're the kind of woman I'm looking to get married to.' They do in Lisdoonvarna, come out with something bold, straight away, no messing about.

'That's a nice thought,' she says, 'but my last husband has only been dead two weeks.' Then she told him she had been married I think it was six times. When he heard that he panicked and ran, and I didn't see him for a long time afterwards.

What this woman told me then was that her first husband had been killed in a motorcycle accident; the second husband caught pneumonia and died of it; why the third one died they didn't know; and with each of her husbands after that, it seemed after a year or so they got into bad health and died, almost as if they created their own psychological sickness, thinking, I'm going to be next. That reminds me of some advice for single men I heard about. 'Remember your good manners,' it said. 'And if you should ever meet a woman who has been widowed three times or more, make sure you always pour your own drinks . . .'

Michael John was one of the local men who very much appreciated the increase in American visitors to the area. Michael John was very refined always. He had worked most of his life in Dublin and London as a history teacher and had returned to the family farm to help his elder brother who was getting on in years. Farming was not Michael John's thing, as he had spent too long in the city, but he worked with the cows and cattle as if it was his duty. His was a very quiet, good family, which was so common in Ireland. One of his sisters had moved to the USA and her daughter was getting married to an Irish boy, so the wedding was held in Clare.

A good amount of American women came across for the wedding. It was a lovely occasion, great fun with a very good band playing. A girl called Coleen, who was a teacher from near Chicago, asked me to find her a partner. I introduced her to Michael John. With a few drinks inside him he seemed to loosen out. Coleen was very impressed with him and his knowledge. She asked him to dance, but he was slow to get up and join her. He said it was his first time. Eventually, with a deal of persuasion, we managed to push him out on the floor for a slow waltz.

When the dance was over Coleen came by and whispered to me, 'Oh my God, Willie, has he got a bicycle pump down his pants or what? Has every Irish man one of those?'

I chuckled and said, 'To be honest I'm not sure, but I do remember it was once said about Michael John's father that he had a weapon on him that would beat an ass out of a bog hole!' Coleen and Michael had one more dance, then another. They became good friends and in due course they got married.

When I saw them after the wedding Coleen was talking about what had attracted her to Michael John, and said she had been intrigued by the breadth of his knowledge. Jokingly I said, 'Now, are you sure it wasn't the bicycle pump?'

Not everything was so great during these years. In 1983, on 27 January, I received some devastating news. My mother and sister Delia had been driving back to Dublin from County Clare after the Christmas break. A man who had been drinking all day long ran his car into theirs. He survived, but my sister, only 41, was killed and my mother, who was 63, died a few days later. There was nothing we could do. The family talked about taking the man through the courts, but I said it would not change anything, 'twas over and that was it. The strangeness of it was that my mother had lost her first husband in a car crash, before she met my father.

I was aware of the property that my ancestors had owned in Dublin 4, the Georgian area of the city, and this now had to be dealt with. I had been made executor of my mother's and sister's wills: the process was long and convoluted and I spent a lot of time in Dublin.

While I was there I was reminded of a story my father had told me when I was a young boy about his own time in the city, a tale involving my grandfather, my father and Michael Collins, the great republican, freedom fighter and politician, who was a regular at my father's B&B and used it as one of his safe houses in Dublin.

My grandfather had introduced a shopkeeper from Ennis to a girl of seventeen, no older than that. The man, in his forties, had a decent shop in Ennis, a hardware store. I suppose the couple got married in County Clare and my grandfather had said, 'My son Henry has a place in Dublin, you could stay there.' This was the little bed and breakfast he had set up in Lower Baggot Street, with a bar and a restaurant next door.

Off the couple set for Dublin. So far, so good. But there was a twist. The girl was a real country lass, a very shy girl who had never been away from her parents' home before. She had insisted that she simply would not go on the honeymoon without her younger brother, who was fifteen, coming too. Well, her husband was far from pleased about this, of course, but she was absolutely insistent, and when he could see that the only possible way he was going to enjoy a honeymoon was if the brother came too, he reluctantly agreed.

The new groom happened to be a fan of the greyhounds, as my father was, so when the couple – with the brother in tow – turned up at the B&B, my father suggested that he and the groom go off to Shelbourne Park, the local greyhound track, for the evening. The bride and the boy were dispatched off to the cinema to see a picture, and everybody headed out about eight o'clock in the evening. On her way out the girl noticed that there was the name of a saint written in tiles in the front doorway of the B&B and she made a mental note to remember it so she would be able to find her way back later on.

My father and the man got back at eleven and had a couple of drinks at the little bar next to the B&B. After a while they wondered what had happened to the girl and her brother, because the pictures had finished at half-ten, but there was no sign of them. So they had another drink, but eventually got so concerned that they called the Guards. They were in luck. It turned out that the boy and the girl were down at the Gardaí station, because when they walked back along the street looking for their landmark, those tiles in the front doorway, all the street doors had been closed and so they had missed the clue. They had been wandering the streets of Dublin trying to find their way back, completely lost and confused, having never been in such a place, though somewhat excited by visiting the city, and the girl perhaps apprehensive about the night ahead.

The girl and the boy got back to the B&B at about twenty to one in the morning. Your man, as you can imagine, was absolutely jubilant. It was the first night of his honeymoon, after all, and at last here was his young bride returned to him. He finished his drink and headed off to find her. But when he went up to the couple's room she was nowhere to be found: she had rushed upstairs and hidden in her brother's room. She had locked the door and she wouldn't come out: she was so shy, and probably petrified of the reality of this wedding night, especially as her husband, with the drink, had become a much louder character than she was used to. The husband started making a terrible din, kicking the door, shouting, 'You're my bride, come out, come out, come into my room,' waking up the whole place.

It so happened that Michael Collins was in the B&B that night. My father was fond of him, a good acquaintance in his quiet kind of way. So it was none other than Michael Collins who met the man in the hallway and brought him back down to the bar to console him: 'You can't be making that kind of noise.' Eventually he calmed the groom down a little, saying, 'You're going to have to take it easy. Give her a bit of time.' Collins also went upstairs to talk to the bride. He was very tall and handsome, and the girl took to him; she felt very relaxed with him, and he persuaded her to talk to her new husband the following day. Calm returned to Lower Baggot Street.

And although it had looked as if the marriage was destined to be a disaster, in the morning the couple resolved their differences. They returned to County Clare and lived together for many a long year, and had a clutch of children together.

Eventually we sold up the properties on Baggot Street, left them behind, and apart from the occasional visit I never went back to Dublin for any length of time at all. The lights of the city I always enjoyed, but I inevitably found myself drawn back to County Clare, to Ennistymon, Ballingaddy and Lisdoonvarna.

Around this time I moved into a new office in Lisdoon-varna, at the Matchmaker pub. When the pub was opened, by the White family, they added a little office in it for me, just inside the door by the side of the Imperial Hotel. They built the space specially for it, didn't even ask me. They said, 'Willie, there's a spot for you right there,' and when they decided to call it the Matchmaker Bar it was ideal. The beauty of it is the location, right in the centre of town. One time I found that they had created a mural of me on the out-side of the pub underneath a banner saying, 'Marriages are made in Heaven, but most people meet in the Matchmaker Bar.' It's still there: myself surrounded by Cupids! It took me a little while to get used to it, although I don't even notice it any more. I'd be a bit of a shy person enough, so initially I was tempted to say I'd rather that wasn't there, but it does pinpoint where it is, and where I am. As long as they don't add too many wrinkles as the years go by, I'll be happy.

I'm fortunate that Lisdoonvarna is a very small town, and everybody who comes in for the festival either passes up or passes down past the Matchmaker, heading for one or other of the venues along the main road. You can't miss the place.

They might be on their way to the Roadside Tavern, which for many years has hosted traditional music: I would spend my early years there with the Curtin family. The Ritz was and is a great spot for characters; the owners, the Crowes, understand people and like to see them having fun. At the

Royal Spa you would always find good music thanks to Paddy Doherty, who produced the Lisdoonvarna rock festivals in the 1980s. The Irish Arms, where I had my first office, is a great traditional pub, and the McNamaras give good dinners and accommodation. The current owner Kevin's father, Joe McNamara, was great fun. Many is the pint Joe and I had together. He was a good footballer, and one day he jumped so high for a ball, he caught a crow instead – or at least that's what he told me.

In the centre of town you find the Rathbaun, with music all day and night, a place that has survived the test of time. The Sheedy family run the Spa View near the sulphur wells, with a good view of the surrounding hills. The Kincora Hotel has been the venue for some great sessions over many years. The Ravine and Lynch's are smack in the main square alongside the Ritz, and again there's plenty of good music, song and dancing. These three hotels attract a crowd of lovely mature people with a great zest for dancing and laughter. I always say the proprietors of Lisdoonvarna deserve a lot of credit for putting on so much music for their guests.

The Matchmaker pub is always busy, full of noise and young people, very different from some of the other venues. And that might put off some of the older crowd, who prefer the quieter, more sedate, genteel surroundings of the Hydro, but because they can see me through the street window as they walk past, and I'm only just inside the front door, they are happy to drop by.

There's no door to my 'office', but that suits me too, because it's open to the general public. The other offices were grand, but too confining, behind closed doors. That was fine when people were inside with you, but there might be good spells of nobody coming in and I'd be saying to myself, Jeez, there's great fun outside, and feeling left out. At the Matchmaker I am behind a table with all my books laid out. There are still a few photos of girls up on the wall. The women are always giving out that there's no pictures of fellas. That stirs a bit of fun.

On two or three of the Saturday nights during the festival, there are times that the noise and heat in the Matchmaker are just unbelievable all right, so if I want to speak to anyone discreetly and privately we can nip into the reception area of the Imperial Hotel next door, which is very quiet.

Anything can happen in Lisdoonvarna. We were in the Rathbaun Hotel one Monday morning, everyone tired and wrecked after a big weekend. It was about eleven o'clock and the music was just starting up again – the musicians don't take much time off for sleeping. Over the weekend I had met four friends, three boys and one girl, who were up for the festival from west Limerick, and we had decided to have a farewell drink before they went home. We got a seat and some drinks, and the first dance had started. This is known by all the fellas as 'the first chance of the day'.

A man rushed over and asked the girl who was with us, Mildred, to dance with him. She was going to say no, as she had a massive headache from all the drinking the night before. But I said to her, 'Go on, Mildred, have a dance with him. What's the harm in a dance?' They went into a quick-step and both danced well. Mildred came back and sat down. Shortly afterwards the next dance started, and the same big man came shooting over again for a second dance. This time he didn't ask her but just grabbed her loose jumper and made a dash for the floor, only to realise when he got there that Mildred wasn't in the jumper.

He seemed surprised at this. Mildred was mortified, as underneath her jumper she was completely topless, and she sat there trying to cover herself up with her arms as best she could. Everyone was laughing and smiling at poor Mildred's plight. The tall man looked at Mildred, tossed the jumper back to her and asked another woman to dance. One of the man's friends came over and told me that he was an energetic, young-at-heart sixty-year-old from Wexford, and that this was his first time going on such a social outing.

Later in the day I saw him again, in another bar. A friend of mine was there too, a great character but mad for Guinness, and always good at telling stories. This time he was telling a story about a local county council worker, a road worker. When a woman walking her dog caught him killing a snail with his shovel, she was annoyed with him and said, 'That's an awful thing to do. Why did you kill that poor snail?'

The road worker replied, 'Ah, he was following me around all day.'

Now the storyteller had brought his small child along with him and was messing with some of the little boy's Smarties. He'd taken all the blue ones out of the pack and was juggling with them in his hand. One of the crowd enquired, 'What are those?' Another man shouted, 'What do you think they are but Viagra, of course. Don't you recognise the blue colour?' Viagra had just come out and it was all the talk at this time. The tall man from Wexford asked, 'Would you sell them?' Well, for another pint of Guinness my friend would have sold the shirt off his back. The man asked again, 'How much?' My friend said, 'Ten pounds – each.' The bargaining went on; it was like negotiating the sale of a horse. Eventually the price of £8.10 was agreed, with a big roar from the onlookers. The Wexford man seemed happy and went off with his three blue 'pills'.

The next day we were in the pub again and my friend was sitting telling another story. He was asking the crowd, 'Why do flies walk on ceilings?' No one could figure out why. He informed them that if someone bought him a pint of Guinness he would tell them. This was done; he actually got three pints from three different people. And then he continued, 'Now the answer why flies walk on ceilings is to take the weight of their feet . . .'

He was just about to start another story, asking who could remember which day summer fell on last year, when out of the corner of my eye I noticed the big man from Wexford coming into the pub. He was heading straight for my friend.

I quickly alerted him and he, thinking he was about to find himself in a fight for selling Smarties as Viagra, tried to make his way out by another door. But the big man reached him first, stretched out a long, powerful arm and grabbed him by the shoulder. My friend looked trapped. In a strong Wexford voice, the big man said, 'Jaysus, have you any more of them pills, they were great!'

11
Believe in Miracles

All kinds of characters come to Lisdoonvarna each year for the Matchmaking Festival. There was one young man who drove to the festival on his Ferguson 20 tractor all the way from Mayo, up north of Connemara. The drive must have taken him an entire day as it was a good four-hour journey by car. When he arrived into town it was a Saturday evening and the place was as usual packed. Coming into town on a Ferguson 20 wouldn't have been all that unusual for a local, but what made him stick out was that he had a scarecrow made to look like a woman perched on the mudguard of the tractor.

There was a sign on this she-scarecrow giving her name, Julia; on the other side of the tractor was another sign that shouted out in huge letters, I WANT A WIFE. The young man was making a mighty racket, sounding horns and blowing bugles. I remember thinking he was quite excited and very funny to see, short with blond hair and a round red face.

He was known as Mickey 'the Hare' Brannigan, and I admired how he planned bringing so much attention to himself. He arrived at the festival at about 9.30 when most people were arriving into town and walking into the pubs. Mickey the Hare blazed into the main street and caught everyone's eye. As he reached the town square he put on a show with his Ferguson 20, turning it fast to the left, fast to the right and then braking hard. Julia almost took an awkward tumble. By now he had a large audience yelling, clapping and shouting, 'More, more!' All night along, everyone I bumped into was talking about the spectacle – but Mickey himself was nowhere to be found. People joked that he'd had great luck with the ladies and invited them straight away to his B&B.

I met Mickey the following day, walking in town. I asked him if he'd had a good evening. He mumbled, 'After the long drive and excitement of arriving in the town, I couldn't keep my eyes open, so I went to bed early.' I felt this was a great pity as it should have been his night. He enquired about the matchmaking, saying he had land and was going to build a new house, which I told him was good. However, that night there was something missing in Mickey the Hare. Without his Ferguson 20 he was a different person. Where he had had a dose of the blarney the night before, it was hard to get many words out of him and sure he wasn't having any luck with the matchmaking. He had been a bit of a celebrity that first evening, but now he was hardly being recognised. Mickey was disappointed how people had cooled off with him without his tractor. At the end of the night I asked him to meet me for a cup of tea at my house the next day.

The following morning we sat down and chatted about farming in general and horses in particular. Finally, I suggested that he go back to his B&B in the afternoon, take a good long nap and then get back on his tractor at around 9 p.m. for a second show. Mickey was a touch hesitant – his original courage had taken a bit of a battering – but he agreed. That night he came down the road and into the square with horns blazing just as he had the first night. Once again the crowd loved it. Those who had seen him before were even more excited, and a gaggle of spectators gathered around the tractor. Four or five girls hopped up on to the vehicle, shouting and roaring, asking if they could have their photos taken with him and his tractor.

That night Mickey was on fire and had a grand time. He was the life of the festival, with endless interest from the ladies. Although he didn't find the perfect woman during Lisdoonvarna, he travelled home with a new-found confidence. He phoned me a few weeks later to tell me he'd met a local Mayo girl and was planning to ask her to marry him. He said the experience in Lisdoonvarna had changed his life.

I hadn't seen Mickey for several years when I ran into him at the market in Ennistymon. He was with his wife in a brand-new tractor, with five kids riding in the cab and transport box. I was so happy for him. We went in to Murt McMahon's bar to laugh and talk about the evening he made his grand entrance on the Ferguson 20. Murt bought everyone, including all the kids, a drink.

Not everyone who comes to County Clare looking for love arrives with such a fanfare. There was one woman, Patti, who came over from the States in the 1950s. She was quite shy, and seemed most comfortable talking to my mother in the kitchen for hours on end, which was unusual because my mother wasn't often involved in the match-making.

My mother and father made a match for Patti with a lovely young fella of thirty-one or so, Brendan, who worked on one of the local farms. My mother set them up a bit, by asking Brendan to walk Patti home one evening. And at the beginning it looked as if it was going to work. The pair seemed to be in love and agreed to be married. The wedding day was named. Then Patti took a short trip to Kerry to visit some of her family's relatives, but she never came back. We got a letter in which she said she was truly sorry, but while she'd been down in Kerry she had met someone else who she liked better. She had decided to marry this other man, and asked my father and mother to apologise to Brendan on her behalf.

Brendan came over to our house one lovely evening and my father took him outside to break the bad news to him as gently as he could. Your man was broken, of course. He really had been in love with Patti. I could see him from my window, head down, crying and asking, 'Jesus, what could have gone wrong? How did it happen? The match was made', and my father saying, 'I don't know,' and he honestly didn't know. He was just as shocked. I think that was the first no my father had got. Although Brendan was heartbroken, he stayed in the area and all was not lost – he eventually married another local woman.

Some romances, sadly, are meant never to happen. When I was about nineteen or twenty there was a period when there were summer marquees all around the area, with bands and dances all night. The summer marquees lasted from May to July at the Family Festival in Ennistymon. The marquees would be there for the whole twelve weeks, offering a sense of excitement at night when they were lit up.

This was just after I had bought my first van, which meant my friends and I could go places. My neighbours Paddy Kearney and Minnie Crehan were also happy for me and said, 'Good for you, Willie. The van will be great for going to Mass and taking the milk to the creamery.'

'It will,' I replied, but I also had other plans, namely getting us to these dances.

One day while I was at the creamery with my ass and

cart a member of the festival committee rushed up and asked a number of us to go down and help urgently. A storm was blowing and the marquee was rising up in the air. It was scary seeing it up in the sky. We helped as best we could and managed to get the marquee under control again. As thanks we were given free passes to dances for the remaining week.

Then I heard that Donnie Collins's band, which had a great reputation, was playing in a marquee at Tulla, about thirty miles from Ennistymon. I had not been to Tulla much, even though I had relations there. The prospect of a new town was exciting, so three of my friends and I went down in the van, my friend Larry driving. Entering a small rural town, we would be treated with a certain amount of contempt by the local boys but they would also be interested and curious.

When we walked into the marquee, I saw a beautiful girl leaning against one of the tent poles. She looked a picture: tall, dark, curly hair and big brown eyes. We danced together and laughed at ourselves, or anything. She told me her name was Irene and that her grandfather was Spanish, which was believable, given her looks. Jokingly I said to her, 'You look very Irish.'

'I am Irish,' she replied, and I said, again jokingly: 'I know.'

Later I walked her outside. It was a lovely summer's night. She told me she travelled with her brothers. As we strolled along she swung about and gave me a most wonderful kiss. Having her in my arms felt good, and I thought a little more of the same sounded even better. Looking for a quiet corner, we went around the back of a tall building for some courting, still kissing, and failing to see a trough of water. There was a splash and then Irene gasping that she had fallen into the cold water. I helped her out, but she was covered in green algae and was soaked wet through. I didn't know what to do. I was speechless, a rare event in my life. Irene exclaimed, 'Jesus, my brothers will kill me.' I thought, If not, they will certainly kill me. We quickly said our goodbyes. Poor Irene. I never saw her again. The song 'Goodnight, Irene' played in my mind for a long time after that.

Like the marquees, going to the cattle fairs was very exciting times. We would take the cattle to be sold out of the field about four in the morning. In the winter it would always be pitch black, and sometimes raining heavily, but there was no choice if we wanted to go and make some money. The banks would not lend a penny to anyone and no one would ask them for money.

By the mid-1960s the fairs in town centres had stopped, and specialised cattle marts had sprung up everywhere. This was a financial loss to the shops in the towns, but the people in the private houses were glad not to have cattle dung all over the doors and walls of their houses. These new marts were about one acre in size, containing cattle pens about twenty foot square. The cattle, each one numbered, would be led into a ring where the auctioneer, buyers and sellers were waiting. A huge difference was that you didn't need to be over at the mart with your cattle until the late morning, maybe even as late as 1 p.m.

On this particular April morning, with a young lad, the son of some neighbours, I set off to the mart about eleven o'clock. We were driving along three bullocks aged around a year and a half. All went well until we hit the main road. If we had been walking along in the dark of the early morning the cattle would not have seen all the turnings and driveways offering alternative routes, and of course there would not have been so many cars on the road. First of all the bullocks ran into a village en route called Killoura. Denny Madigan, a good friend of my father's who lived there, helped us round them up again, and decided to come along with us. As we left the village, he remarked, a great saying of his, 'God of glory, the cattle were always wild coming out of your place.'

We headed towards Ennistymon where the mart was. As we drew near the walls on one side of the road were about eight feet high. Two of these bullocks climbed those walls. It was difficult to imagine how this happened; it seemed nearly impossible because the walls were so high, but they were determined animals. After a great deal of running around we eventually got them back on the road.

We were now entering the town itself. Something had gotten into the three bullocks, they were going mad. The face of the little boy with me was as red as a turkey cock's from all the exertion, as mine must have been too. Denny was still with us and now another man, Tony Curtis, had joined us too. We passed O'Brien's hardware and grocery shop. Next door was Mrs Byrth, a seamstress sewing clothes: her shop was small and also served as her bedroom. A narrow corridor led into the house and lo and behold two of the bullocks went straight in her door. I was flabbergasted, but I had to get them out.

The bullocks had gone right into Mrs Byrth's shop-bedroom. There she was, sitting up in the bed, her sewing machine in front of her. She was crossing herself and saying, 'Will they kill me? Will they kill me?' I tried to reassure her by saying, 'It will be OK. We'll get them out.' The bullocks were at the foot of her bed, their breath like a steam engine from all the running and dashing. I quietly walked across Mrs Byrth's bed and very slowly nudged the animals back out of the room. It was scary as they were really wild now and anything could happen. Somehow I managed to edge them to the door on the way out. One jumped right over Mrs Byrth in her bed and fell on the lino on the floor. He scrambled up and made for the front door. My heart was in my mouth.

But worse was to come. We were proceeding up Main Street when one of the bullocks made a rush for Burke's pub, straight in the front door and behind the counter, which was stacked with glasses turned upside-down to dry out from the night before. Mrs Burke ran out on to the street, speechless. I could see her trying to say something like 'What in the name of God is going on here?' but not managing to get a single word out.

Her husband Ned stood tall in the kitchen, just looking on. As I walked into the pub as gently as I could I saw the bullock looking out from behind the counter at his two companions on the pavement outside. This is where the danger lay. He was looking through a huge plate-glass window. My main concern was that he would decide to come straight through it to join his friends.

I gingerly put my right hand over the counter to edge him back so he could get out. I was so lucky again, as he did reverse. Behind the bar was too narrow to turn. At any moment he could still plunge forward again and dive through that big window. He was going well, swinging to the left, putting his backside out of the gully he had come in by.

There was a fire going in the very corner of the bar. The bullock touched the fire with his nose, went back like a shot, swung to get out of the door and sent one pint glass – but only one – crashing to the floor. Now that truly was a miracle.

Denny Madigan ran ahead to Parliament Street and asked all the shops to close their doors, but the three bullocks escaped again and went into the classroom of the monastery just beside the cattle mart. The kids found this hilarious of course, though the Christian Brothers were shocked. They lent us five boys to help us get the animals to the mart, some three minutes away. As they entered the cattleshed at the mart, Tony Curtis remarked, 'Willie, whatever you get for those bullocks, sell them!' And I did. I must have gone to hundreds of fairs through the years, but I never came across the state those animals were in.

In the end just one shilling's worth of damage was all they had done, and I thanked God that old Mrs Byrth or Mrs Burke had not suffered a heart attack. It was a massive intrusion into their homes. They were great about it, and some time later we laughed about the events of that day.

A small drop of matchmaker's advice

♡ *Something happens in the Irish countryside in the spring. It's like a young calf coming out of the shed for the first time. People are out and about, crowding the pubs – they're mad for action. It's a period of newness where there's great possibility for finding love. The seasons played a very important role in the lives of the early Irish Celts, and they are still important to mark time here in the west of Ireland. I really enjoy the matchmaking in the spring and find it very easy to make a match because people are emotionally open. I believe this is true all the world over.* ♡

Shortly afterwards I met Mick and Patrick, two brothers who'd waited a good long while to turn their minds to marriage, but after their mother died they both decided this was the time to get married, and they got in touch with me. I invited them to a dance in Ennistymon, and told them I would be there too. The dances were great fun but there was always a shortage of women. When the men came out of Cassidy's pub at half-eleven or twelve and into John O'Neill's guesthouse for food, they would easily outnumber the women.

So these two good old boys rolled up. I don't think they'd ever been much interested in dancing, but they were adamant that they wanted to find a wife. I was taking a turn on the dance floor myself when I saw the pair of them talking to a couple of young women at the far end of the hall. Sheila and Jane were two lovely girls in their early twenties, over for Easter from London, where they both worked; I'd pointed them out to Mick and Pat when they arrived. They were obviously asking the girls to dance with them, but I could see the girls laughing and shaking their heads – I guessed they wanted to dance with some of the younger lads.

But the brothers kept talking to them, and it turned out that they had told Sheila and Jane they were really interested not just in dancing but in getting married. Eventually the conversations led to two engagements, and Mick and Sheila, and Pat and Jane, got married on the same gorgeous summer morning. Because someone had to look after the cattle, the couples took it in turn to go on honeymoon. Off went Mick and Sheila down along the coast to Kerry, and three days later we heard that Mick had died. But, as my friend Brendan O'Malley the undertaker told me, 'At least Mick died with a smile on his face. You could tell he was having a good time because it took us three hours to hammer the coffin lid down.'

When I was a boy there was a local storyteller called Peadar who had a tale about a woman with twenty-five children. He would tell us that her husband, Sean Og, was vague. I would think to myself that he couldn't be that vague to have twenty-five children. As the story unfolded, Peadar would relate that Sean Og was a bit older than his wife and had a bad back. 'Some men would say it was no wonder his back was bad' – at that time I didn't understand the joke. Peadar would say that when the sun would appear, Mags, the wife, would say with a vengeance, 'Jesus, a fine day is a blessing,' as it would get all the children out of the house. The little boys were often dressed in girls' clothes with their hair long, as Mags was worried that the fairies would steal the boys away. Sean would sit outside with them and count the children, and then count the plates for dinner.

Mags washed clothes for a living at a big river near her house. At this point my mother would interrupt Peadar and ask him, 'How did she dry them in this climate that's always raining?' Peadar would say she was always singing and laughing and happy.

Peadar continued: 'Sean Og was old' – I was amazed why they called him Sean Og, as this meant 'Young John' but later I learnt it was to identify the father from a son and grandfather of the same name. 'Sean Og became ill so the priest came to anoint him, to help him make his peace with God and get ready for the road to Heaven. After being anointed, Sean Og improved for a while and called Mags into his bedroom. She took him in a cup of tea and biscuits and sat on the side of the bed. Sean Og said in a faltering voice, "Mags, I want to thank you for having been a wonderful mother and wife. There was a big age gap between us and it couldn't have been easy for you." She put her hand on his and said, "'Twas grand, 'twas grand."

'Mags was about to go back into the kitchen to fetch a damp cloth to cool Sean's forehead when he called her back. "Just one more thing, Mags. You know how all the children have dark hair except Jimmy with the red hair. Am I his father? I would like to know before I leave you all." Mags thought for a while, took away her hand and hung her head. "Am I, Mags?" he repeated. Raising her head slowly she said, "You are definitely Jimmy's father, Sean, but you're not the father of the other twenty-four . . ."'

And if you believe that story, next time you come to our little corner of the world I will personally introduce you to the family of leprechauns who live in the valley of Ballingaddy. And should you happen to meet them first, just tell them you are a good friend of Willie Daly, the matchmaker of County Clare.

12

The American Dream

After all the dreams I had, growing up, of going to America to become an entrepreneur, a pop star or a film actor, I didn't go to the States until I was into my fifties. That was unusually late in life, given that so many of my family, my friends and neighbours, along with half the rest of Ireland, had travelled there, casting one last farewell look towards the Clare coast before setting out across the Atlantic.

Now for some reason, when I was in my late teens and early twenties many more of my friends were choosing to go to England than America. Perhaps the glamour of Liverpool and London in the 1960s was more appealing for those few years. A number of the girls went to work as nannies and housemaids, were treated very well and as time progressed were eventually looked after in turn by the children they had raised. These Irish girls were so good with the babies and the young kids that they were almost more of a mother than the actual parent in some cases, and the children would retain a strong bond with them for the rest of their lives. Not many of these girls married, though. It was said that very often one of the men in the house would fall in love with the lass – these girls had a particular gentleness about them, a bewitching mix of shy sweetness with great loyalty that was very sought after – but would end up marrying somebody else, someone from more of what they'd consider their own league.

But for the generations before, the dream was America. Lord have mercy, an awful lot of my mother's family went there. And whenever another young fella or girl decided to leave for America, oh, there would be a farewell wake and a half, and going-away dances that would be brewing for a couple of weeks. There would be great merriment, at the very same time as it would be terribly sad for the mother and father and the families and close friends. In those days there was no television, very few phones, hardly any cars, and a family would all be living terribly close to each other, very close knit. They had their neighbours, but there was no big wondering what was down the road forty miles away; you could imagine it, but that was as far as you'd go. It was nearly a walking world, very intimate.

So when somebody would be leaving, the family and the friends they had been to school with were naturally in a very sad mood, but before then there would be a great build-up of music, a good bit of drinking involved, and there might be a certain amount of fights would go on. Somebody might have made up a batch of thirty bottles of powerful poteen and supplied a handy bottle or two of whiskey and a raft of bottles of beer. At that time the women generally wouldn't drink, though they might try and have something on the quiet. But the men would be as drunk as a skunk, drinking all night, getting awful rowdyish at times, and the singing and dancing always brought out aggression in some. It was always an excuse to sort out rows between certain families about who was the strongest and toughest.

A lot of old women would be there, bawling and crying, drinking on the sly as well. I'd say some of them had little in the way of remorse in them, since they were no relation of the family. There was a couple of them as were called wailers, who would be invited, as in the funeral wakes, to say the rosary: they were nearly professional criers. They'd start off sobbing, and everyone would join in.

These dos would go on till the following morning. You'd have a number of married couples with younger children, as there was no thought of babysitting, and they'd head off, maybe the wife at half-one or two, then the husband might stay till four. The single fellas would carry on till the morning, trying to dance with the girls and go courting outside, not heading out of the door together, mind you – no, they were very subtle like that. You'd never see two going out holding hands; the boy would head away out first, and she would come later and he'd be waiting round the corner of the house for her and off they'd go into a cowhouse.

Those were not the only goings-on during those nights. There would be a few young lads out to create mischief, especially on party evenings when the family were charging a few pence for coming in. There'd be a lot of fellas trying to get in for free, as not many would have the penny. 'Twould be a challenge to get in. And if they couldn't, they'd decide to get their own back. They'd be right little blaggards, but innocent enough – there'd be nothing vindictive. The old houses often had a porch and it would be very easy to hop up on to the roof. These vagabonds would get up on top and stuff the chimney with straw and place a stone flag over it. Next thing, within the house the smoke would be coming down and out, and everyone would start to cough. The family would have to put out the fire, but they couldn't throw water on it, because it would have blasted the ashes up on top of them. They had to carry everything outside with tongs, and it might take a good half an hour to sort everything out and get back to the craic.

There were all manner of different agendas going on at these parties, and there could be four or five new relationships coming out of it. The fellas were not as slow as they usually were. They'd know this kind of party might not happen again for another six months or more, so they would make the most of it. Hence there was an awful lot of excitement about these American wakes, as this was an occasion that had all kinds of social consequences and ramifications, especially where there might be seventeen girls in a house and maybe fifty fellas at the party. It would be talked about for two weeks before and for a long time after.

Certain men, whose families had no reason to attend, would even ask whether their daughters or their sons could go; they might dress it up under the heading of how they'd like them to learn how to do the dancing.

The house would be tiny, the place would be packed. And like the plucking of the gander you'd find the older women up teaching the girls how to dance, trying to get them used to fellas' ways, tickling them, pinching them close, a certain form of preparation for what might be coming at a point in time. Some of these older women might feel they were losing their own appeal to men, and for some of them there would be an element of frustration, their husbands that much older, no sex any more in the relationship.

If the girl who was going to America had a steady boyfriend, there might be a room they'd spend a good bit of time in, and us younger lads would be looking in through the keyhole of the door or there might be a little knot in the timber, the usual curiosity, of course. Oh, there were all kinds of possibilities and excitements going on, if you knew where to look.

After all that, in many cases the boy or girl, particularly if it was a girl, would not actually go to America! All of a sudden, at the very last moment, they might change their mind. Everything was ready, the ticket there on the sideboard, and then the truth of what they were about to do set in. It was very common that it would dawn on them just how far a distance they were going to be away, which at that time – before satellites and global communications – it really was, and often no prospect of returning to Ireland at all. They might come home only after ten years; some never came back.

If it was a girl who was going, it was often the father and mother secretly hoping – and that's why they would organise the wake – that something would develop over those final two weeks; that a local man would realise, God, I'm never going to see Bridie again, and at least propose to her. But equally it might not work out like that at all. It might be too late. There were girls going who had built up a certain picture in their minds of what life in America was going to be. When I was young, neighbours of ours who had been to America would come to our house and we would all attentively sit and listen to their stories. Now they knew that no one wanted to hear a bad story, so they'd tell great tales and paint marvellous pictures of the wonderment that existed in New York or Boston or Chicago.

And once that image was fixed in a girl's mind it was hard to budge. Maybe a year or five months before that she would have gladly said yes to a proposal, but now this idea of being out in a new, glamorous world had outstripped the prospects of being married to a man at home that mightn't be good-looking. Perhaps if there was a very good-looking man she was in love with that might be different, but otherwise she'd be getting married for the sake of having a home, and maybe a small little old home and a little old man, and she'd made up her mind, no, she was going.

I often heard my mother and father talking about a man who had been going out with a girl for a good while, and when he had come to a final decision to ask her not to go to America but to marry him and stay in Ireland, she had turned him down. 'Jesus, he was heartbroken,' my father would say. 'God, 'twas a shame that he left it to the last minute to decide.' The other picture had got bigger than him: a year ago his little house would have seemed a mansion but now she'd heard all about these skyscrapers in New York, the huge stores, people with loads of money and a great social life, a whole city full of lights and dazzlement. (Sometimes, of course, when they finally got there, the reality of the New World was not quite so wonderful as they imagined.)

The fellas left behind might regret it for the rest of their lives. My father would see them out and about. 'Why did you let that lovely girl slip through your hands and go off to America?' he'd ask.

That was the legacy for these rejected suitors, and the mothers and fathers, torn with grief as they saw their lovely son or daughter heading off, would quietly know that they might never again see them. Now it's all much different – you can fly out there in eight hours or less – that aspect has gone. But when I was growing up and listening, it was all about the grief.

The reports would come back: 'Ah God, the mother was in an awful state.' The fathers generally would say nothing. Oh, they'd be feeling it considerably, but they would keep it tucked away within themselves. And while there was a deal of grief there would also equally be an acceptance that there was no choice and that their child would be in a better world. Things were awful bad, the Lord save us, coming up out of the 1920s and 30s, and before that it had often been worse.

On the road between Lahinch and Ennistymon is a memorial to those who lost their lives at the Union Workhouse; a reminder of the dreadful toll during the Great Famine of 1846–52, when 80,000 died in County Clare. Those were *an Drochshaol*, the Bad Times.

When the sons and daughters did go, they would be leaving by boat, some via Cork, but many from this area set off from Liscannor, the very bay I can see from the kitchen window. The boats stopping at the harbour there were picking up Liscannor flags or stone, the bread and butter of this area, before heading on to London and New York. The crew on board would strike up friendships with the local men working on the flags, and a number did decide to leave after talking with the crew. Some of the lads would work below decks on the boats to help pay for their passage, and the girls might help with the catering.

There was a lot of sailing ahead of them, not far off two or three months to arrive, which must have been very trying, an endless amount of loneliness for many of them from off these hills, who would never even have been to Ennis or Limerick, only in their own house with their parents and all their sisters and brothers; they'd be seriously missing them a lot. I always felt it must be an awful culture shock for them to arrive in New York, so busy, so bloody busy, and so full of people and no face they knew.

A small drop of matchmaker's advice

♡ Much like those young Irish neighbours who dreamed of skyscrapers and of discovering their fortune in America, I frequently come across people who have similar grand expectations in love. Those young immigrants who were often met in the New World with few opportunities and loads of rejection were not unlike the modern singles here in Ireland today. Naturally a person can become discouraged when they don't have instant success. As I said earlier, I think the first step to finding love is to be ready for it. The second step is to accept that you will experience a bit of rejection or disappointment from time to time. If you didn't, you wouldn't be human. Finding and starting a relationship takes time, and you have to be patient. ♡

The children of those who went to America often stayed and did not come back to Ireland, but for some reason their grandchildren and now the great-grandchildren of those friends and neighbours who left for America do often visit to discover the land of their forefathers. And when the next generations return they usually say, 'God, this place is beautiful, why didn't we come back sooner?' And like Phyllis, the girl from Boston who met my friend the fiddle player Michael, they might not just find their roots but love too.

But not all. Tony was a quite awkward and fidgety man in his forties who came to the Lisdoonvarna festival for a number of years. He lived somewhere out near Cape Cod and had a very strong affinity for all things Irish. I thought we had struck lucky during his very first visit when I introduced him to the perfect Irish girl he had always dreamed of, a girl from Dublin called Kiera. They hit it off great and spent three nights dancing and talking together.

When it was time for Tony to fly back to Boston he was devastated at the thought of leaving his new love, so he made a plan to send her a plane ticket a few weeks later. When he phoned her to firm up the plans she revealed that she had not told him she had a son from an earlier relationship, and that this boy would also need a plane ticket. Tony did not hesitate and purchased two tickets direct to Boston. Kiera and her son arrived a few weeks later and immediately moved in with Tony. At first things were exactly as he dreamed. Tony also became very fond of her son and felt a strong bond with the lad. However, Kiera soon started going out on her own in the evenings while Tony stayed at home babysitting the boy.

A few months went by and then Kiera announced she had

fallen in love with another man, who was also Irish, and that they were moving back to Ireland. Tony was heartbroken and tried to convince her to stay. Alas, it was not in the cards. Tony returned to Lisdoonvarna for the next five or six years, but has never found anyone to replace the love he felt for Kiera. Matchmaking, you see, is an imperfect science. You can sense the potential for love but not always see the kinks in the road ahead. My success rate is pretty good, otherwise I'd have long found myself out of a job, but they do say only the Pope is infallible.

My first visit to America was a less traumatic event than Kiera's trip to stay with Tony. I was invited to a spend a week in New York centred around a matchmaking day. I was so busy before going out that I only really thought about the trip when I got to the airport. At Immigration they stopped me and asked where I was going.

'New York.'

'Have you friends out there then?'

'No, I'm going to a festival.'

'And where are you staying?'

'I have no idea!'

I was just being very honest with them, and they were hesitant enough. But then I remembered that I was carrying my grandfather and father's matchmaking ledger. I brought it out to show the officials. They got intrigued and sure enough they did let me through.

There must be some remnant of the spirit of William and Henry Daly lingering in the faded ink on those yellowing pages. The book seems like a lucky talisman. That's why I keep it close by at all times.

As it turned out, I was staying on 29th Street in Manhattan, just over Paddy Reilly's pub. In I walked and lo and behold I met about six or seven musicians who had all played in my pub in Ennistymon, and other friends I knew from County Clare. They were terribly pleased to see me, and I them. Paul Hill, the fella who married Bobby Kennedy's daughter, was the first I met. He had often come into our pub. It was like home from home.

My other big surprise was that, after friends in America had told me, 'Willie, you have to be very careful in New York walking around, try not to give the impression you're a tourist,' I went all over on my own, or with one or two people, at three in the morning and never had any trouble.

Our day arrived. It was a Lisdoonvarna festival sponsored by a Guinness promotion, all based around Paddy Reilly's, the Black Sheep and maybe two or three other bars. I went down at twelve and the festival was really kicking, not least thanks to the free beer. (It was free for me, at any rate.) The whole of the block was closed off and there was a trailer with some very good Irish music playing. They brought me up on to this stage about one o'clock and I talked about my life as a matchmaker and told everyone I would be available to help with matchmaking for the next while.

The feel was like a younger version of Lisdoonvarna, especially with the amount of Irish people from Liscannor, Ennistymon and Kilfenora, from my own parish of Kilshanny, all now living in New York. I'd known most of them in the past, and even met two distant relatives of my own. It made me realise the serious amount of Irish who were in America that I knew; or if I didn't know them personally, I knew their family.

I even got some matches going. I introduced a fella I knew to a gorgeous girl from Mayo, very voluptuous and sweet, who he later married, which I was very happy to do. This fella would have been Irish-American but had spent a lot of time at home, close to where I was. They both sat with me that evening with some more local people, from Liscannor mainly, and a few from Ennistymon.

Whiskey was my drink of choice at the time, and everybody I met wanted to buy me a glass. In the entire week I spent there, I only got to buy one drink myself – and even that they wouldn't let me pay for in the end. On the Sunday morning of the day that I was flying home, I was in a pub up around Harlem. I'd gone off to explore by myself. I had my tin whistle with me and was playing a few of my tunes. I bought a bottle of beer and as I was finishing it, the owner said to the barman, 'Did you charge that man for the drink? Give him back the money. He's a musician.'

*

A little later I was invited over to America again, this time to Memphis, by some of the fellas who used to organise a barbecue festival in Lisdoonvarna, including Mark Flanagan. Mark is a regular character in Lisdoonvarna, and here he was running a St Patrick's Day parade, not anything as big as there is every year in New York or Boston, but large enough. Once again I had no idea where I was staying. I forgot to get the details as there was plenty of spring work to do on the farm. It was nearly impossible even to get away. The immigration desk was suspicious again, of course. But I had the old matchmaking book with me, and between laughing a bit and being serious, they let me off anyway.

And as I came out of the airport I realised I had not made any arrangements to meet my friends. I thought, What am I going to do? It's eight o'clock at night and I haven't got a clue where I'm meant to be going. I walked out of the terminal anyway, and as soon as I stepped out this band struck up, fellas dressed up as leprechauns with beards and giant shamrocks. And there of course I saw the friends who had invited me over, Mark Flanagan and Silky Sullivan, who they call 'the most famous Irishman in Memphis'.

After the band had played for a while we decided to take off. There were about ten or eleven cars. I was in a huge white stretch limo with three motorbikes at the front, three more at the back. I thought, Even John F. Kennedy wouldn't have this kind of a welcome.

Every day that week we would go to a different pub or a

café as part of the festival. And then in the evenings Silky Sullivan would invite us to one or other of the nightclubs he owned. For one of them he had brought three or four goats over from Ireland to Memphis, and he'd crowned one of these goats King of the Festival, just as they do at the Puck Fair in Kerry. On St Patrick's Day itself we went to Mass, where the priest told some stories, and I told a few more about priests and leprechauns. And the main parade that day was louder, longer and more flamboyant than any of the other celebrations, over which I had the honour, though I didn't think I really deserved it, of being the Grand Marshal.

A couple of nights afterwards Mark and Silky and another friend of theirs, a local judge, decided to take me to a casino down on the Mississippi River. I had quite an interest in casinos – maybe something I inherited from my father, who did like a bet on the cards or the greyhounds – and was keen to go, but before we reached the roulette tables, we were taken to see a show version of *Moulin Rouge*. The next thing I knew we were being ushered up to the best seats right at the front. Later I asked the others, 'Do you mind me asking how we got up there?'

'Ah, we told them you were the President of Ireland!'

13

Love in the Twenty-first Century

There have been moments during the past twenty years or so, I have to admit, when it crossed my mind to wonder whether the tradition of matchmaking had had its day, and whether my role as a matchmaker might become obsolete.

Since the time when I started matchmaking there have been greater opportunities for most people, and especially women, to run their own lives, to take decisions about their future. The days when families dictated who their children should marry – and likewise who they could not marry – were long gone, and thankfully so. I would never stand in the way of anybody's independence; I've been fiercely independent my whole life. But if they were determined to make their own choices, who would ever want the help of a matchmaker?

With the digital revolution, chat rooms and dating

websites took off, yet another challenge to my way of working. Life became hectic in a mad way, and the relaxed environments where a couple could spend time together and build a relationship seemed thin on the ground. It's all rushing, rushing, rushing, though many people never seem to get that far.

I had been through my own turmoil, too. Marie and I, I am sad to say, separated towards the end of the 1990s. Our lives together, once so bound up, had been stealthily unravelling, and I had been too busy and too blinkered to notice until it was way too late. Not only was I now coming to terms with a life apart from the mother of our children, but I found myself an older single man again, exactly the kind of fella I had spent most of my adult life trying to help! I really started to wonder whether I should give it all up and spend all my time with my horses.

And yet, at the turn of the millennium, somewhat to my surprise and great pleasure, I found a revival of interest in matchmaking. Here I am, in the twenty-first century, and as busy as I have ever been. Every day new requests for help and advice find their way to me somehow or the other. My phone never stops ringing, and with the arrival of e-mail and the Web people can contact me at any moment of the day. The Matchmaking Festival continues to grow each year. I'm still going strong, and maybe that's because I have always been able to adapt to the times.

In 2007, during the festival, a large group of twenty

couples came into our pub on the main street in Ennis-tymon. They were all in their late twenties and early thirties, a young and vivacious bunch. I knew a few of them and put my foot in things by asking without thinking who was married to who. Quickly one of girls said, 'Come on now, Willie, you're the matchmaker, aren't you? You tell us who is with who.'

I wasn't mad about doing this, as it's very easy to get the couples wrong. Mind you, even if you do get it wrong, that can be fun as you always get a good laugh by pairing them off wrongly. I felt this was a challenge and decided to do it to the best of my ability. I surprised myself, and got about seventeen right and only three wrong. Later on one of the girls who I had put in a wrong couple came over to me and quietly told me, 'Willie, I wish it was as you said, but that's life . . .'

A small drop of matchmaker's advice

♡ *Now I don't pretend to be a wizard at the computer. My daughters have been good enough to help me keep up with the times by setting up a website for me, and I do get a lot of enquiries by e-mail. I think that's because it's a fast and easy way to communicate. I can see the attraction of finding love on the computer. It's like magic! You answer a few questions and hey presto! – a list of people who are perfectly suited to you. Now, I am sure there have been great romances started on the computer, but eventually there has to be a face-to-face meeting. I think it's only natural that a person would invent a person they aspire to be. But this is fantasy and can be hurtful to all when the truth comes to light. I wouldn't say a person shouldn't try the computer dating, but I would make certain you are getting out and meeting people in real life as well. You can't hide behind a keyboard for ever.* ♡

So I ask myself why; what is it that matchmaking offers? It is nearly needed more than it was going back thirty years. There must be something deep at its heart that offers re-assurance and belief. It's like Irish traditional music. Thirty years ago, there was great talk of it disappearing into thin air: no one would be interested in reels and jigs when they could listen to U2. Yet now there is a great resurgence, a renaissance of traditional music. The melodies and rhythms had rooted themselves deep in the landscape and, with a little care and the new interest, have flourished once again. When you come to visit, just go down to one of the pubs in Doolin, O'Connor's or McGann's or McDermott's, and you'll find a session going on pretty much every night. And if you play the whistle or the fiddle, bring it along and join in.

I think the sense of reassurance and old values is a great part of the matchmaking. For single people the dating game is a real confusing little arena these days. One girl said to me not long ago, 'Willie, it is very hard to meet a nice person.'

'I'll agree with that, it is.'

'Yes,' she went on, 'if I go out to a dance now' – she was thirty-five, I'd guess – 'I want to dress up good and respectable to create a reasonable impression. But at the dances we go to there's usually a substantial amount of separated women. They swan in with their top down low and their skirt up high and the fellas are enticed by that. It seems like they've learned twice as much as they did the first time round, and on top of that they carry a certain spirit of vengeance as well. It's hard to compete.'

You can imagine these gentle, respectable girls in the centre of that, getting lost in it; it's tough for them. You would not believe the amount of gorgeous women who get in touch with me and would dearly love to meet somebody nice enough. When they find that little bit of love, it's a great feeling for them. All that is there for them in our traditional matchmaking.

With the Internet dating sites, I've learnt not to feel in competition with them, if I ever did – they only prove to me that there's a need for somebody to act as a matchmaker. But 'some*body*' rather than 'some*thing*' is the key word. It is obvious that computers are machines, and machines are very impersonal and cold. They have no feelings, no heart or soul, and they don't understand the emotional situations people have or the pain that might exist. Most people have no idea what they really want in a partner, so how can they tell a computer the characteristics of the person who is going to be their perfect match?

And do you know what? Although I have made a few changes to the way I do the matchmaking, the usual stuff – the mobile phones, my own website – the truth is that what I really do hasn't changed at all. The mixture of experience, humour and hope is still there. And if life has become more frantic, well, you should pitch up at the Matchmaker pub on a crazy Saturday night and you'll find out what frantic really means.

Although there is a percentage of women in Ireland who might feel they have moved on and wouldn't need to consult me, I still find that there are many, many men looking for the spirit of those Irish girls of time past, the ones who either were content to settle down with a husband on a farm, or who left to go to England as nannies and brought a special gentleness to the families they lived and worked with. Many people hanker for what they saw as more innocent times. I can understand that feeling.

Over the past few years I have seen the arrival here of some lovely girls from Thailand and the Philippines. They come from a tradition of courteousness, and are often looking for a calmer, stable relationship with a man who owns some land. At first I was surprised when these elegant girls in their twenties told me that they weren't really interested in men their own age, but I grew to understand that they wanted something more genuine and long-lasting. They prefer a more subdued person, and some of the older local men, who have lost a bit of the steam of their younger days, equally appreciate that same gentleness that was once typical of the young Irish girls who went over to England to work as nannies.

Sometimes men are simply frightened by the change in attitudes. I was over at a horse fair down in County Kerry the other year, and a man called John Boyle came over to me, who said he'd heard I was a matchmaker. 'That's right,' says I. He told me he was now in his forties and had a small farm with four or five cows, making a modest enough living, and wanted to settle down. Could I help? He didn't have a phone on this farm, but I promised to leave a message with his sister if I came across a suitable girl. In the end I invited John to come up to Lisdoonvarna during the Matchmaking Festival.

When he turned up I said I'd found a suitable girl for him, called Eileen, who was over from Dublin for the festival with three of her friends, a grand foursome, all in their early thirties and good-looking. I met the girls in one of the pubs in Lisdoonvarna and sat waiting for John with them, while a number of fellows came over to chat to them, because they were a high-spirited bunch. Eventually John came in, and Eileen clearly liked him. I bought the group a few drinks and everyone was on good form, dancing away. After a half-hour or so John offered to get everyone a drink, and I was delighted, because I liked his gentleness and was glad to see him having such a good time. Off he went to get the round – and he never came back, just disappeared. Eileen must have noticed, but there were so many other fellas ready to buy her a drink, she moved on.

A month or two later I bumped into John at another horse fair. 'John, what happened? You were getting on so well with Eileen in Lisdoonvarna and then you vanished.'

'Ah yes, Willie,' he said, 'she was a lovely woman. But when I asked what everyone wanted from the bar, she was drinking vodka' – 'wodka' was the way he pronounced it. 'Wodka! So I hoofed it out of the door as fast as I could . . .'

John was an old-fashioned country man, who was used to the men drinking together in the pubs and the women maybe drinking lemonade or water. These city girls from Dublin had shocked him. Funnily enough, Eileen asked me about John a little later on, and asked if she could see him again, but when I got in touch with him he still said no: 'I just couldn't see a woman who drinks wodka, Willie.' Although I often believe that opposites attract, this was something much deeper, something essential to John's whole personality, so I respected his decision. But another part of me thought he should maybe have relaxed a bit – the last time I heard, he was still single . . .

Finding love can be difficult and unexpected, but that is its beauty. I am always fascinated by the unpredictability of love. If it was too scientific then I wouldn't enjoy what I do so much, and we might as well leave the whole job up to the computer. What you can't build into a dating program, of course, are the wonderful oddities of human nature.

An old fellow in his seventies came back to Ireland after living and working in Japan. He'd returned with a much younger Japanese girl, in her twenties, but she then found her independence and left him. He got on to me to meet a woman, and I introduced him to a couple of possible partners. One was a Chinese woman in her forties who lived in Dublin, but when he met her she was wearing a very short mini-skirt. His heart started racing, and he had to go into hospital. When he was better I introduced him to another girl and she was dressed in a low-cut top, and his heart started going again . . . 'Jesus,' I said, 'he's not giving up though.' He rang me from the hospital twice! More power to his elbow.

A small drop of matchmaker's advice

♡ *An awful lot of men dream about getting married, and then the minute they get close to a woman they panic. They tend to pick on something beforehand to find fault with, that her nose is too big or her hair is too long. My father used to have a saying about these fellas: 'The woman isn't born yet that they'd be happy with.' I'd notice the difference in the men on the eastern coast of Ireland, around the Dublin side, they were often too picky and fussy; whereas down the west coast they'd be totally opposite: they'd be quite relaxed in Kerry, Cork or Clare. They wouldn't want to meet someone instantly, whereas on the east coast they'd join today and nearly want the woman yesterday. 'Willie,' they'd ask, 'isn't there a girl near?' and I'd say, 'Jesus, if she was that near, wouldn't you get her yourself?'* ♡

In 2008 a television company from Holland got in touch with me with a new idea funded by the Irish tourist board, Fáilte Ireland, to promote the country by showing off all the good-looking fellas in Ireland, along with the most pictur-esque landscapes. The plan was to bring three girls from Holland – Sophie, Esther and Muriel – to seven different destinations. My part in the programme was to introduce each of the girls to seven suitable boys, one from each of the places they had chosen. The girls would generally be staying in castles or old houses in deliberately romantic settings.

Kinsale, a small port down in County Cork, was our first stop. The three local men taking part, Barry, Michael and Robbie, each took one of the girls out on a date. There was sailing, painting, a round of golf and a picnic. Kinsale is always very beautiful, but we were having lovely warm weather that summer and it looked particularly stunning. The girls need not have looked any further than these three lads, but the production crew of course expected them to meet the other men I had lined up.

So we went on to the next destination, Killarney in County Kerry, another lovely part of Ireland, full of lakes. And again any of the three Kerry men, Henry, Dermot and Andrew, each very handsome, could easily have been the right one. One of the guys took Esther out for a spin on the jaunting cars; Sophie was taken rallying; Muriel adopted a lamb and was taken dancing.

After Killarney we made for a stop in Tralee, where the Rose of Tralee is crowned every August. Here Muriel learnt how to surf and had a great time with a lad called Brendan. Sophie went out with Patrick on a horse trek, but Pat was a little preoccupied: he was very much into hurling and couldn't stop talking about it. Esther's date was called Ciaran; he arrived on his motorbike, swept Esther off her feet and took her diving – their date ended with a candlelit dinner. Again these three guys were great potential husbands, but the girls still were not allowed to make up their minds.

In Ennis, where we headed next, I had a difficult process deciding who should go out with the girls, because Ennis is in my own county. I knew the three men personally, and very well at that. Clare men often get quickly involved romantically and emotionally with a woman, and I felt that one or all of the three girls could be proposed to by the end of the day.

Esther had another adventure with a motorbike on her date with John. This one wasn't so successful, though, as she fell with the bike, but bravely enough she got right up on it again. Richard and Sophie had a lot of fun. He showed her his particularly beloved part of Clare, the Burren, which she seemed to enjoy very much. Muriel and Shane enjoyed themselves surfing and relaxing at a traditional Irish night in Bunratty Castle. I think all the boys proposed marriage to the girls that time; they seemed besotted. But curiosity kept the girls going as they were only halfway through the journey.

So off we went to Recess, an area of forests and lakes in Connemara, breathtakingly beautiful. There was fly fishing and horse-riding on the beach with lovely Connemara ponies. One couple, Esther and Michael, flew across to the Aran Islands; they took the boat back with a group of kids going back home to the mainland after three weeks on the islands learning Irish. The kids encouraged them to be more romantic and have a kiss, the little matchmakers.

We moved northward to Ashford Castle in Cong, County Mayo, where Dez took Muriel out for a spot of clay-pigeon-shooting. She turned out to be a natural with the long-barrelled gun and hit all the clays. Cupid played a good part and took a shot at both their hearts.

The final destination was where else but Lisdoonvarna. The three girls met their last dates in front of the Match-maker Bar. I was very relaxed at this point, since of course this was where I do most of my matchmaking. These seemed to me to be three matches made in heaven. Ross took Muriel to see the old Ireland; Mark and Sophie had an indoor pro-gramme of bowling, snooker and an evening taking part in a *céilí* at John Vaughan's in Kilfenora, famed for the Irish dancing that takes place there every Thursday and Sunday night. Meanwhile John took Esther to view the Cliffs of Moher from a different angle, walking down the old goats' trail before sampling a seaweed bath at the old spa wells in Lisdoonvarna.

Decision time was close. The girls had been out with seven different good-looking men; now they had to choose just one. How they could choose one out of the crowd of their magnificent seven and condemn the rest to cold oblivion, I don't know. But fair play to the three girls, they made their choices. Esther settled on John, who she'd met in Ennis, and Muriel chose Shane, who'd taken her surfing. Sophie made a radical decision to choose Ireland as her match, rather than one particular man. Esther and John became very good friends; Muriel and Shane kept in touch, but decided to go their own ways. And Sophie, who chose Ireland, left her home in Holland and moved permanently to County Clare; for her it was the perfect match.

14
The Shadow of the Sycamore

When I walked up on the hill behind the house in the early-morning sunlight on that day I decided to take up matchmaking seriously, I was very aware that I would now be the third generation of Daly matchmakers. As I get a little older – but only a little, mind – each year, I wonder if there will be a fourth generation. Different years, newspapers have reported I'm retiring, though I'm still hard at work, but I know there will come a day when I have to wind down and give it up.

In front of the old farmhouse next door there once stood seven magnificent sycamores, marvellous tall trees. One day in the autumn of 1961 a terrible wind, Hurricane Debbie, blew in from the Atlantic. She was the worst storm we had ever seen in the west of Ireland, and she felled the sycamore nearest the sea. The tree had sheltered the rest by taking the full force of the gale. A few years later another storm took out the next of the sycamores. I think of those sycamores as the line of Daly matchmakers. William has gone, my father Henry followed. I am the sycamore closest to the buffeting winds, and I will do what I can to protect the next in line, but after a while they will have to stand up for themselves.

Memories of my grandfather and father are never far away. The other year I made a match for an old farmer nearby, who I met at a horse fair. He had a good personality, was well spoken and reminded me strongly of my father in the latter end of his years.

And recently I was stopped in town by an old man who wanted to tell me about a good turn that William had done for this fella's family, at the turn of the last century. His family, the Brennans, had been evicted from their home after the husband had died, and the widow, left forlorn with seven children, wasn't able to pay her rent money to the landlord. She was from Ennistymon, so the priests tried asking at the Ennistymon and Kilshanny Masses if somebody could provide a house for her.

My grandfather heard about their plight and immediately went in and said he would give them a place to build a house. He got together the parishioners with their horses and carts; they cut all the timbers from the trees round here, brought in stone, trimmed straws for the roof, and the very same evening the family were able to move in. Wasn't that some achievement, for a house to be built in one day? The house is mostly gone now, but the site is still there, marked by the green of the bushes where the road peters out. I am hoping to restore it myself one day soon.

My children have very mixed feelings about whether or not they wish to carry on the Daly family tradition. Most have helped me out at some time or another, so they know what being a matchmaker involves, the good and the bad. It won't be up to me to choose. A matchmaker, as they say, would have a charm for the job.

My daughter Marie was the one who at first seemed to have the most natural talent for matchmaking and helped me a good lot for a number of years. There came a point where it seemed she might have outgrown her interest, though that could swing around again in the future. Claire, my oldest daughter, who also has a great way with people, was very good at matchmaking but didn't have time to do it when she started a family and was looking after her small children, although recently she started talking about doing it again.

Henry is a blacksmith, and helps me in the riding business, but he has also dabbled in the matchmaking. In fact, I remember watching him as he made his own first match. Let me tell you how it happened.

Pamela was a local girl, a shining light, exciting, full of fun, a film-star type. She had all the fellas after her, and why not – she was our Marilyn Monroe. Living in a small town didn't provide enough opportunities, and she went to the USA when she was twenty or so, but she would come back regularly for holidays: she had a house in a small village outside Ennis.

When she was back home she often came to our riding centre, always a breath of fresh air, creating sunshine even on the wettest of days. I would ask her, 'Well, Pamela, any big romances?'

'Oh, loads, Willie,' she'd smile back.

'Your problem, Pamela, is that you have too many men to choose from, and you can't decide which is the right one.'

She'd say, 'I'll soon be asking you to find me a solid farmer.'

We'd laugh, as I could not see this happening, because her life in America seemed far too exciting. But one day she called me. 'Willie Daly, can you find me a farmer?'

I said, 'Of course I will,' though I wasn't sure if she was serious or not. But she was coming home to Ireland after fifteen years away. That's great, I thought to myself, as a day out of Ireland is a tragedy for any Irish person.

Sure enough, she arrived back, and the next time she came over to ride one of the horses her first question was 'Did you find me that man the farmer yet?' I asked her why she wanted a farmer, and she said she wanted to grow a garden. For a moment I thought about all the different types of men she had known and I told her, 'You're right. I admire your decision.'

'Willie, you know me, I've had my fill of all those time-wasters and fools. And I love nature and the countryside round here.'

We went off for a ride and came across a man and his wife out tending their garden. Pamela stopped and talked to them for some time. She was obviously intrigued by every aspect of gardening.

We came back to the house for tea. Henry, with my younger son Rory and a couple of their friends, were in the kitchen – four bachelors who needed to get married, they agreed. 'You're all lovely,' said Pamela, 'but you're too young.'

Rory, being smart, said, 'Why don't you marry Willie? He needs a housekeeper.'

'I'd be glad to, but he's too old!'

We sat laughing and messing about, then Henry said, 'I have the very man for you.'

'What's he like?' asked Pamela.

'He's a farmer, very romantic and full of life.'

'Henry, cut the crap, does he have a garden?'

'Well, he has a great garden but he only uses a tiny corner of it now.'

It turned out that although I didn't know this fella, Andy, I knew his parents. He lived not far away in Miltown Malbay. Henry was due to shoe one of Andy's donkeys later on that day, so Pamela agreed to come along to meet him. 'You'd better glamorise yourself up for Andy,' said Henry. 'He's used to glamorous women.'

Pamela went off to change and arrived back looking gorgeous. As she got into Henry's van, she insisted I go along too. We arrived at Andy's farmyard just as his mother was letting the bull out to one of the cows; the bull did his business twice in five minutes. It was quite a welcome. Andy stood there, red-faced and smelling of farms, cows and all their attendant fragrances. Pamela was laughing at the carry-on. The bull didn't want to leave the cow, so he was allowed one more bit of fun, and then quietly strolled back to his paddock.

When Henry introduced Pamela to Andy, he was very direct: 'Pamela wants to marry you.' I nearly passed out at Henry's bluntness. Andy's face got even redder as he coughed and stuttered some kind of reply. Henry, being on a roll, repeated, 'Are you going to marry her or what?'

Andy's voice started at a whisper and then out came the loudest 'Yes' I ever heard. As Pamela and Andy sat and talked, I could see him pointing out to her where the garden was, full of rich, black soil.

The wedding was a marvellous event, with a jazz band playing, quite unusual for rural Ireland. Pamela told me it was the one thing Andy had insisted on.

A year passed, and Andy rang Henry to come back and reshoe the donkeys, so I joined him for the visit. As we arrived, Pamela shouted to us from the garden. It looked as if she had all of it cultivated and she told us she was sowing cabbage plants. Her hands and clothes were black from the soil. She was very happy, and informed us she was seven months pregnant. 'Andy's in the house,' she said; 'go on in.'

We pushed the old door open and shouted hello. 'I'm here in the study.' We followed Andy's voice and found him sitting at the desk in front of a computer – 'I'm Googling shares,' he announced. He was actually quite reluctant to leave the computer and fetch the donkeys for Henry to shoe them.

Pamela joined us at the shoeing, and she and Andy talked for a while, then she headed back into the old farmhouse and returned with a pale blue envelope which she handed to Henry.

'What's that?' he asked.

She pushed it into his pocket and said, 'It's a gift for you, for making our match.'

A small drop of matchmaker's advice

♡ Someone wise once remarked that if you constantly carve a new image of yourself, you will eventually whittle yourself away. There is great truth in this. Do not underestimate your own life experience – draw on it. Everyone has a story, because everybody's life has taken unexpected turns, twists and forks along the road. Tell your story and you will find someone who wants to listen, and then let them tell you theirs. ♡

Henry also organised a speed-dating event during the Lisdoonvarna festival, at the Imperial Hotel. There was great enthusiasm. It was hilarious. The idea was for couples to sit and talk and then move on after five minutes. But you'd get characters who wouldn't budge, then you'd see a couple kissing each other only two minutes after they met, and they wouldn't move out of their chairs. What can you do if they're happy? You can't force them to cooperate. When that happens they've met their match. Of course other fellas were getting grumpy, and started jumping a few places. It was mayhem, but great fun, just right for the mood of Lisdoonvarna. I've been to one or two other speed-dating events and it was like going to Mass, so religiously done, there was no fun in it. No one seemed to be meeting anyone in particular. And the fellas wouldn't have enough of a drink in to make a pass at a girl; they'd be too apprehensive.

Of course it would make me pleased if one of my children continued the tradition. The surprise may be that my youngest, Rory, might be the one to do it, though he hasn't yet got involved. Rory has a marvellous outsize personality, a great zest for fun and craic. I had a huge surprise one night when he went to a fancy-dress dance as Tina Turner! I wouldn't have had the courage. I was amazed but delighted.

To this minute Rory has shown no interest in match-making, but I know he likes the glamour of it. A couple of young girls came down from Dublin making a documentary about older bachelors living in County Clare, and he showed a lot of interest in those two girls, anyway.

I'm not looking for an apprentice. If Marie or Claire, Henry or Rory want to stay working at the matchmaking, they will find their own way of operating. And I will watch and do my best to protect them while they find their feet.

Whichever Daly it is, their matchmaking style will be very different from mine. For example, Henry is not fond of all the pulling and the dragging that happens during the Lisdoonvarna festival. When the festival is on, and people get to drinking, they don't care what you're at, they want your attention at that moment. You can't say to someone, 'Sit down there and I'll be over to you in five minutes.' You have to listen to them then and there. That's grand for me. I enjoy it. I never had a problem with the constant demands. It never seemed to be any bother. But if you're sitting with someone else, they can get upset.

And there's a large percentage of those people who want your attention who are messing, three-quarters drunk: 'Willie, Willie, Willie, Jeez, get me a woman.' You just have to smile a lot and say of course you will and tell them, 'Come on, come in here a minute.' They're in company with friends, so they act flamboyant and I know that and that's a nice thing, an admirable thing in a sense. Half the times if you introduce a woman to them they nearly run away. They don't expect it to be done. They like the roaring and the messing and the blaggarding, but when the woman is produced they don't think it's going to happen. Now all that banter and carrying on isn't anything that's difficult to handle. But it's not to everybody's taste. So, time will tell if I am the last of the Daly matchmakers. God willing, I won't need to find out for a good long while.

Now before you go, let me tell you one last story.

A few years ago a group of people came into my pub in Ennistymon; it was quite common for visitors passing by on their way to Lisdoonvarna to pop in for a drink en route. My daughter Grainne was behind the bar and came over to tell me, 'Pops, there are some people over here who want to say hello to you.' I looked over to where she was pointing. There were perhaps six or seven of them, all ages. A man in his fifties came towards me, saying, 'Willie, do you remember me?' – to be honest I didn't, but I waited – 'I'm Jamesie McGrath, from near Silvermines in Tipperary. You introduced me to my wife Mary twenty-nine years ago. We had a great life together. Now my son Michael is here with us and I'm wondering whether you might have a fine woman for him too.' His son, a big, strong young fella, was watching us from the end of the bar. I wondered what he was thinking. So I said what I say a lot: 'Of course I will.'

There were a couple of musicians in the pub. They played for a few hours and I could see Jamesie's group of family and friends enjoying themselves and obviously feeling very much at home. This evening was going well. It was a typical Irish party, slow to start but with the alcohol gaining fury. Three American women wandered in a little later on in the session, and again Grainne caught my attention. 'Pops, these three ladies up here want to meet you. I think they're looking for husbands.'

I went over to talk to the ladies, Peggy, her daughter Megan, who was a sweet girl of twenty-seven, and a friend of Peggy's called Caroline. Peggy said, 'You are Willie Daly the matchmaker, aren't you? The landlady at our B&B said we might find you here. We're all looking for husbands.'

'Three good-looking girls like you will have loads of men chasing ye around the fields,' I told them.

As we were chatting, Jamesie, well lubricated by this time and a little unsteady in the legs, approached with out-stretched arms, dancing to the music, and pulled Peggy out to dance. The musicians were playing 'Under the Bridges of Paris': 'Oh, what I'd give for a moment or two . . . I'd make your dreams come true.' Jamesie and Peggy waltzed off into the middle of the pub.

Someone else brought out Caroline to dance, and Megan was left on her own, so I asked her out to waltz. We talked and laughed as everyone was bumping into each other. The space was small, but so much the better. On our way back to sit down I introduced Megan to Jamesie's son Michael. She accepted the introduction gracefully, but I thought Michael could have tried a little harder. He was an imposing figure, but dour and looked like a fish out of water, especially as he wasn't drinking because he was driving.

I didn't say too much as I felt the timing was wrong. Jamesie and Peggy on the other hand were having a ball. After what was a great evening of frolics, fun and leaping about to the music, they got ready to leave. I heard Michael giving out to his father, saying, 'You're making a clown of yourself. It's a long time since *I* had that much fun.'

Jokingly I told both of them, 'This Guinness is great stuff. It creates magic!'

Jamesie stepped back and with tears in his eyes told me, 'Willie, Mary died three years ago this fall. I'm very lonely. Will you talk to Peggy for me?'

I said I would: 'I'll meet you in Lisdoon about nine-ish, then.'

His face lit up.

Lisdoonvarna later that night was packed with people, young and old, all looking for fun and romance. Nine o'clock passed and I hadn't seen either Jamesie or the American women. About ten o'clock Peggy, Megan and Caroline came into the bar. It was the first time they had been exposed to the exuberance and mad atmosphere of Lisdoonvarna. They seemed a little shocked by the volume of people. As they sat down, they looked as if they needed some time to adjust to the size of the crowd. I suggested they get a few whiskeys to help them adjust.

While Megan was making her way to the bar, Jamesie,

Michael and the rest of the gang were coming in the door. This was a different Michael from the one I had met earlier on in Ennistymon. The Guinness had worked its magic on him. Happier and more outgoing, he stood there with a gleam on his face, swinging his cardigan over his head. He looked larger than life in more than his size. When he caught sight of Megan he rushed over to her, didn't ask her to dance but lifted her up in his arms and ran to the dancing area with her.

A man standing by the door of the office had taken a great shine to Peggy and asked to be introduced to her. As I was about to do so, Peggy excused herself to go to the ladies' room so I introduced him to Caroline instead. He brought Caroline out to dance. When Peggy returned Jamesie asked her to dance, but she said, 'It's awfully crowded here. Shall we go to a less crowded place?'

I suggested the Ritz might suit them. 'Go ahead,' I told them. 'I'll tell the others ye have eloped!' They both laughed and off they went.

I was busy enough in the office. Some time passed and the others, Megan and Michael, and Caroline and her partner, hadn't come back, which I thought was a little odd. When they eventually returned from dancing I told them where Jamesie and Peggy had gone. Later on I went up to the Ritz myself and was very happy to see all three couples still together and happy and dancing.

I met them again the next night; they told me they had all

been up to the Cliffs of Moher where Peggy's hat had been blown into the sea. Jamesie said he would take her in to Ennis the next day and buy her a new one. I told them, 'The old hat will probably be back in America before Peggy,' and jokingly Jamesie said, 'Peggy's not going back. She's staying here with me and we're getting married.'

'Is that a proposal?' Peggy asked.

Jamesie said, 'It is.'

Megan looked at Michael, said, 'I guess we'll be seeing a lot of each other then,' and they tore out to dance.

I happened to be in Ennis the following day and saw Jamesie and Peggy across the street. I crossed over and asked had the new hat been bought. Peggy said yes and that they had bought something else. She showed me a lovely ring with an emerald stone. A few weeks later, on the day of Jamesie and Peggy's wedding, Michael and Megan found me and showed me their own engagement ring. Michael surprised me by thanking me for introducing Jamesie to Peggy, saying he had never seen his father so happy and that he and Megan were mad in love as well.

And if that's not a happy ending, I don't know what is.

Acknowledgements

I would like to thank a lot of people who were marvellous in helping me to write my story. It seems like only yesterday I was sitting in my kitchen telling stories to Anne Lanier, who said to me, 'Why don't you write a book, Willie?' And here it is! Anne has consistently encouraged me and helped me find the perfect group of people to make the dream come true. I feel lucky to have had Philip Dodd to help me put all my stories on paper. I am very grateful for his support and talent. I am also thankful to Gordon Wise and Antonia Hodgson for their professionalism and guidance in getting my book published.

To my wonderful family and the many, many friends that I have made throughout my years of matchmaking, horse-riding and socialising, thank you for all the great times.

My family, who have always given me their unrequited love and trust. A very special thank you to Marie, the mother of my lovely family. To my children, Claire, Grainne, Marie, Henry, Elsha, Rory, Sarah and Pascale. My grandchildren, Jack, Oonagh, Ava, Anna, Ciaran, Isaiah, Finn Bob, Saoirse, Gabriel, Cassidy, Talulah, little Elisha and Marlon.

My dear mother and father, sisters Delia, Elizabeth, her husband Sean Ward and children Robert, Tara, Colm, Eimer and David. My half-brother Michael Cashen, his wife Betty and family. Bobby and Ailish Dwan; Joan and Katie; Eileen and all the Kellys in Galway and the Ambroses of Kileedy in County Limerick. A very special thank you to Noreen Egan for her love, kindness, patience and assistance on this adventure and looking forward to many more. Thank you also to Peter McGuigan and Hannah Gordon at Foundry Media; the entire Little, Brown family, especially Hannah Boursnell; Kara Welker and Generate; Shaheeda Sabir and the Curtis Brown family; Kent and Mary Lanier; Dara Molloy; Joanna, Wan Mae and Mei Mae Dodd; Margaret Hasenzahl and Marian Sheedy.

Thanks to my great neighbours for all their help and kindness – the McMahons; the Kearnes; the Crehons; the Houlihans; the Meehans; the Commanes; the McNamaras; the Davenports; the O'Rourkes; the Cullinanes; the Scaleses; the McInerneys; Pat and Mary McMahon and the Madigans – Joe Shannon, Paudie, Phillip and Martin. Thank you.

For all my friends from the early years through to my golden ones – my great friend Noel Meehan for all the fond memories of our shared youth together; Pat O'Leary; J.J. Gallagher; Vincent Kearney; Bill O'Brien; Paddy Fitzgerald; Francy Murphy; Larry Shalloo; Michael O'Doherty; Jerry Maloney; the Mee family; the Conlons; Eddie Stack; Pat and Donal O'Looney; Seamus Donnelly; Gerry Keane; Mona and Gus

Davies; the Droneys; Michael and Willie Stackpoole; Johnny Organ; Paeder Barrett; the Woods family; the Conoles; the Howleys and John Vaughan of Kilfenora. My Lisdoonvarna friends the Drennans; John O'Neill; Gerry Flaherty; the Dohertys; the Crows; the Connollys and John Petty. A big thank you to the Whites, Marcus and Jim; Patsy Whelan; Ted Furey and Micilin Conlon, my musician friends at the Roadside Tavern, *fadó, fadó*; my good friends Mark Flanagan and JohnJoe Scanlan. Thanks also to the Nestor family of Cahermore, Kilshanny, who helped with the hay. Kathy, Steve and Sarah Elovich from Connecticut; Anne, Hugh and Leslie in Liverpool; Paddy and Debbie Burke in Dublin; the O'Connor family; the McGanns and the McDermotts of Doolin.

For my close friends that have passed away – Sean Kelly; Noel Meehan; Paddy Daly; John Keaney; Michael Frawley; P.J. Kenealley; John and Michael Nestor; Minnie Crehan; Ellie Kelly; Kate and Paddy Kearney; Lorcan O'Connor; John Kearns and Agnes Charbon. *A Dhia, tabhair aire do gach duine sna bhflaithis.*

My matchmaking assistants Aisling, Amy, Georgina and Katie. A very big thank you to my good friends Michael Fitzpatrick, Frazer Brown and Marion Cliff. My cousins Sean Kelly and James O'Gorman; Willo; Liam O'Dwyer; Thomas Crehan; Michael Ambrose; Breda Shannon; Anne Gallery; Pat Nestor; James O'Meara; Chris Lynch; Lottie, Michael and Pat Kearney; Oisin Burke and his cousins; Sophie Heusy and Marie Hynes.